RGN May 21 2012

The Sheep of His Hand

REFLECTIONS ON THE PSALMS
FROM A 21ST CENTURY SHEPHERD

SUZANNE DAVENPORT TIETJEN

MONARCH
BOOKS
Oxford, UK & Grand Rapids, Michigan, USA

Author's agent: Books and Such, Inc, 4788 Carissa Avenue, Santa Rosa, CA 95405

First published in the UK in 2009 by Monarch Books
(a publishing imprint of Lion Hudson plc),
Wilkinson House, Jordan Hill Road, Oxford OX2 8DR.
Tel: +44 (0)1865 302750 Fax: +44 (0)1865 302757
monarch@lionhudson.com
www.lionhudson.com

ISBN: 978-1-85424-894-7 (UK)
ISBN: 978-0-8254- 6298-6 (USA)

Distributed by:
UK: Marston Book Services Ltd, PO Box 269, Abingdon, Oxon OX14 4YN;
USA: Kregel Publications, PO Box 2607, Grand Rapids, Michigan 49501

Unless otherwise stated, Scripture quotations are taken from the Holy Bible, New International Version, © 1973, 1978, 1984 by the International Bible Society. Used by permission of Hodder & Stoughton Ltd. All rights reserved.

This book has been printed on paper and board independently certified as having come from sustainable forests.

Cover photograph by Michael Hucal III.
Illustrations by Fred Apps.

British Library Cataloguing Data
A catalogue record for this book is available from the British Library.

Printed and bound in Malta by Gutenberg Press.

Contents

4

Acknowledgments

I'd like to thank the members of my flock and the farm community who helped our family when we were new to keeping sheep. We had a lot to learn and these gifted teachers (animal and human) were patient with us even when we must have looked like idiots.

I'm very grateful to my daughter, Bethany, the first shepherd of our flock, and my husband, Mike, who does all the heavy lifting. Both of them have done their time in Shepherd School with me.

To my agent, Janet Kobobel Grant, thank you for zeroing in on my need to focus this work and for your valued advice along the way.

To Tony Collins and the publishing team at Lion Hudson/Monarch – it's been a joy to work with you. Thank you for your patience with me.

Finally I want to thank my fathers – human and heavenly.

My dad, Whit Davenport, has always believed in me and been there when I needed him. Daddy, I love you.

God, you are so present with me in the barnyard and when I sit down to write. Draw me close to you and never let me stray.

Introduction

When my daughter arrived at Moody Bible Institute on move-in day, a young man from California complimented her on her hand-knit sweater. She informed him that it came from the wool of her two favorite sheep, Sancho and Baab.

His head snapped around in a classic double-take. "You have sheep? Where are you from?"

"Here in Illinois," she said. "I live on a farm."

He stopped and stared. "They still have those?"

Yes. They still have those.

Today's Christians are several generations removed from the family farm and eons away from the sheep-based economy of Old Testament times. When even serious Bible students read passages about sheep, their minds entertain the *image* of a sheep rather than an understanding of a real one.

I did the same before I became a shepherd.

I figured I had a pretty good grasp of my relationship to God and his to me.

I didn't know what I didn't know.

People in Bible times didn't have that problem. The

humble sheep, *ovis ammon aries*, played a huge role in their lives. Sheep provided food (meat, milk, butter, and cheese), warmth (clothing, floor and wall coverings), shelter (pelts and felt structures), and conveniences (soap, candles, musical instruments, and more). Sheep were central to a person's standard of living, with the size of a family's flock being a measure of their wealth.

The Shepherd's Psalm resonates with our hearts, but we remain strangers to the rhythms of the pasture, the habits of sheep, and how they perceive their world.

God says we are his sheep.

David's generation got the meaning.

Do we?

Although most of us have never confronted a sheep face to face, we are enchanted by the idea of them, so much so that images of them decorate our socks, sweaters, and home furnishings. Babies are introduced to them in their earliest picture books. Children cuddle toy sheep when they go to bed. Pastoral scenes of grazing ewes and leaping lambs comfort our hearts, hinting at peace – so elusive in our hurry-up world. Their gentle beauty draws us to the sheep pens at the fair. Leaning in to touch them, young and old delight in the softness of lamb's wool and smile in surprise at the sweet scent of lanolin clinging to their fingertips.

Despite their reputation as "not so smart," sheep have a great deal to teach us about ourselves and our relationship to God. Like snowflakes and people, sheep are all different. They can be contrary or cooperative – caring for them is a challenge. In fact, shepherding was God's prerequisite leadership course.

Abraham, Jacob, and Moses tended sheep, and before David was crowned the Shepherd-King, he spent many years in shepherd school. His skill in managing the flock equipped him to lead a nation.[1]

My sheep, like his, are excellent teachers. I've discovered more in the pasture than in any classroom about myself, other people, and my walk with God. It's a rare day that I don't learn something spiritually significant from watching and working with my wooly friends.

That's why I wrote this book. So you can learn from them too.

Like us, sheep have faults. They can be destructive, rebellious, and greedy. Their fears overwhelm them. They're helpless on their own, yet fight to get their way. They blindly follow bolder sheep, but don't foresee consequences. Every member of my flock is an individual with a name, a personality, and specific needs. Timid, trusting, or somewhere in between, each has a story.

Sheep – like people – are what they are.

Their greatest weakness – their tendency to follow – can be their greatest strength.

I often wonder what God really expects from us. Knowing how often I disappoint and misunderstand him makes me think it must be something fairly simple. Possibly something even a sheep could do.

Look at the way Jesus called his disciples when he gathered that little ragtag bunch. What did he ask them to do?

Study me?

Understand me?

No.

None of these.

He said, "Follow me."

That's what he asked his disciples.

It kind of surprises me that they did.

Jesus said, "Follow me."

They dropped what they were doing and went.

Jesus didn't stop with calling the twelve disciples. He calls to us – each of us – to follow him daily.[2] He echoes the call of God to his people through the ages: "Oh, that my people would listen to me! Oh, that Israel would follow me, walking in my paths."[3]

That cry is the heart of the Christian walk.

Over and over again Jesus calls us – you and me – to follow him.

Will we?

"Come to me. Follow me."

But how?

We don't know how.

We find ourselves frustrated and disappointed with a Christian walk marked by self-effort. We're tired of trying to please God by keeping a list of rules, believing the right things, wearing that Christian mask – in short, trying to "get it right."

So how *do* we follow Jesus?

And why is it so hard?

I have great news for you.

It doesn't have to be.

Come.

Meet my sheep.

Walk with me through the pasture gate and into the Psalms.

And learn from the experts what it means to follow the shepherd.

Bought for a Price

Fifteen years ago our family left the nomadic existence of the military to settle down on the family farm in central Illinois. Bethany, the youngest, was especially excited. She talked about joining 4-H (an agricultural youth organization - the H's stand for Head, Heart, Hands, and Health). Her new friends had beef and dairy cattle, black-faced sheep, rabbits, and poultry. I tried not to influence her choice too much, but I was hoping she'd decide on sheep. I had always dreamed of keeping them, spinning their wool, knitting sweaters, and learning to weave. Sheep seemed like good creatures for a fifth grader to raise. We learned that they were gentle, required little in the way of labor on a daily basis, and because of their absolute reliance on a shepherd, would instill a sense of responsibility in our daughter.

As it turned out, Bethany fell in love with sheep. We spent hours reading about various breeds and looking at pictures. Bethany talked with her 4-H leaders and friends and made her decision. She would be a shepherd.

Now all she needed was the animals themselves.

She decided to start with black sheep, because natural-colored wool is rare and commands a higher price from fiber artists. She checked the classified ads in *The Black Sheep Newsletter* and *Sheep* magazine. We went to auctions and fairs. With every contact, the sheep charmed us. Once I had to drag Bethany away from a petting zoo where she had bonded with a little white lamb (I still have a picture of the two of them, heads bent toward each other, foreheads just touching).

Finally she found an ad placed by a shepherd in Wisconsin whose husband insisted she downsize her flock. Bethany counted her hard-earned chore cash, overcame her fear of the telephone, called the shepherd, and struck a deal. Her dad made rails for the pickup and we set a date to drive north to choose her sheep. Even the snow drifting across the isolated two-lane roads didn't dampen Bethany's enthusiasm. She fairly bounced on the seat every hour of the journey. Her eyes widened when she stepped inside the barn, and she was transported by the unfamiliar sights, sounds, and smells into the ageless world of sheep. She tried to remember what to look for when she chose her two ewes from the pen of yearlings (she later admitted that she couldn't help but fall in love with their faces rather than judging them on sound structure like she'd been taught).

Her dad loaded the little ewes into the pickup bed and we set off for home, imagining how our silent barn might someday ring with the sounds of sheep, the wood burnished to an oily shine from the wool of hundreds of sheep.

That's how we started. And now our barns are full of life and noise, sorrow and joy, the wood indeed polished by lanolin and time.

It began when we loved and sought the sheep. The sheep didn't know we existed. They certainly didn't seek us out. My daughter saved her money. She located the sheep she wanted, traveled to them and chose the first sheep in our flock. She counted out the wrinkled bills and bought those sheep for a price, then took them under her care.

The sheep didn't seek the shepherd. All too often, given any choice in the matter, most sheep try to get away from shepherds – scattering, getting lost, and placing themselves in danger. Sheep, like people, enjoy thinking they're in control, but they are never in more peril than when they are on their own.

Instead, and always, the shepherd seeks the sheep. He owns them and they are his. We, like the sheep, would be better off if we lived like we believed this.

Look at this: look who got picked by God!

PSALM 4:3, *THE MESSAGE*

He is our God; and we are the people of his pasture, and the sheep of his hand.

PSALM 95:7, KJV

Dear Lord,
Thank you for seeking and choosing me.
Help me to understand that I am yours and you care for me.
Help me to want your will and not my own.
In Jesus' name, Amen.

16

Now follow...

God often compares his people to sheep – we are the sheep of his pasture – the sheep of his hand (the hand in this case implies protection and guidance as well as declaring that we are sheep he himself cares for rather than assigning our care to somebody else). Our family too, personally cares for our sheep. Some of them seem content to belong to us, while others remain wild and independent. This week, when you start to make plans and chart your own course, stop and be reminded that you are not your own. You were chosen by the Shepherd. Ask him to lead you – and then follow.

But Aren't Sheep Stupid?

This is every shepherd's most frequently asked question.

Some shepherds answer "Yes."

I don't.

Sheep may look stupid because their only defense against predators is to run away. But they aren't stupid; they're reactive. When flight is all you've got, you use it quickly and without forethought – after all, there's not much to think about when you only have one stunt in your repertoire.

Worse still, the sheep's sole strategy doesn't always work. While I was writing this chapter, forty sheep in Spain were killed by a pack of three dogs. A few of the sheep had been bitten, but most of them died trying to escape. The sheep, many of them pregnant, piled up on each other on an area of high ground and suffocated.

If *anything* startles a sheep, it bolts – sometimes even into inanimate objects. It's hard to look brainy when you just ran into the side of the barn.

But don't judge them too harshly. Let me tell you a few stories about sheep intelligence and you can decide for yourself.

My friend raises Suffolk sheep. They are beautiful black-faced sheep – stylish and… smart. Debbie feeds her sheep in the same order every day and each sheep has its own feeder. At dinnertime, they stand up one at a time and casually walk over to the feeders right before their turn. They don't get up as soon as they see her coming, or when they smell the grain, but when they are next in line.

Now, her husband feeds these same sheep in no particular order. When he puts out the grain, the ewes crowd his knees, pushing and shoving to be sure they get their share. Not only are these ewes smart enough to remember their feeding order, they also recognize each shepherd's feeding style and adjust their behavior accordingly. Pretty intelligent, don't you think?

The BBC reported a few years back that sheep in the Yorkshire moors learned to cross eight-foot-wide cattle grids by rolling across them commando style. The grids were installed several years ago after free-grazing sheep were held hostage by a Marsden gardener when they threatened to devour his vegetables. Eyewitnesses are quoted as saying the sheep are "quite clever," and, so far, the villagers have been unable to devise an effective way of keeping the hungry animals out of their gardens.

A spokeswoman for the British National Sheep Association said, "Sheep are quite intelligent creatures and have more brainpower than people are willing to give them credit for."[4] Richard Cobb, sheep expert from the University of Illinois, ranks sheep "just below the pig and on par with cattle in intelligence among farm animals."[5]

Our ewe, Pigeon, proves his contention – she is an ovine Houdini. We've walked around and around our fencelines trying to discover her secret exit, without any luck. She, like the sheep on the Yorkshire moors, laughs at five-foot fencing, going wherever she wants to go whenever she wants to go there. If I thought sheep were stupid, she would have me wondering where I ranked in farm intelligence.

A common denominator in all these smart sheep stories is motivation. Sheep are smart about what concerns them, from their perspective. Sheep can figure out a way to get something when it is something that *they* want. They don't really care about the state of the gardens in Yorkshire or the plans of their shepherd. They know what they want and, if they can, they'll figure out a way to get it.

I'm the same way.

I make plans based on my own desires. Doesn't everybody?

I expend a lot of thought and energy getting what I want in life. I don't see this as a problem because I don't see the consequences of my choices. David – psalmist, shepherd, and king – recognized that he wasn't smart enough to decide on the right course of action. He leaned instead on God's Word to guide him, saying, "God's Word warns us of danger and directs us to hidden treasure. Otherwise how will we find our way? Or know when we play the fool?" (Psalm 19:11–12, *The Message*).

When we recognize that we aren't as smart as we think, we can be led by God. David said, "I was totally ignorant, a dumb ox in your very presence. I'm still in your presence, but

19

you've taken my hand. You wisely and tenderly lead me, and then you bless me" (Psalm 73:22–24, *The Message*).

I've heard several pastors say that when God compares people to sheep it's not a compliment. Maybe not, but taken in context and seen as a whole, God's relationship with us parallels that of a shepherd and his sheep. He is a good shepherd, *the* Good Shepherd. And while we're no mental match for him, he understands and makes use of our native intelligence.

We must use that intelligence to realize that we need a shepherd. And, like David, we ought to run to him and trust him to teach us how to live.

> If you are really wise, you'll think this over – it's time you appreciated God's deep love.
>
> PSALM 107:43, *THE MESSAGE*

> Be blessed, God; train me in your ways of wise living.
>
> PSALM 119:12, *THE MESSAGE*

Heavenly Father,
Thank you for your love and concern for me.
Help me think before I react when I am threatened.
Remind me that I can't see the whole picture
and shouldn't make decisions
based only on what makes sense to me.
Teach me to seek wisdom in your Word
and trust you to lead me gently by the hand.
In Jesus' name, Amen.

Now follow...

This week, pay attention to those times when you unthinkingly react. A loved one's cutting remark, a careless driver cutting you off in traffic, or a boss's public reprimand may set the stage. We, like the sheep, may act without thinking when we are threatened.

How do you defend yourself?

Sarcasm?

Anger?

Frozen silence?

Ask God to show you how to respond to situations like these in ways that are pleasing to him.

Precious

To love at all is to be vulnerable. Love anything, and your heart will certainly be wrung and possibly broken. If you want to make sure of keeping it intact, you must give your heart to no one, not even to an animal. Wrap it carefully round with hobbies and little luxuries; avoid all entanglements; lock it up safe in the casket or coffin of your selfishness. But in that casket – safe, dark, motionless, airless – it will change. It will not be broken; it will become unbreakable, impenetrable, irredeemable.

C. S. LEWIS[6]

Shepherds' hearts are tender and often broken.

We care for charming, willful creatures. And, yes, we love the sheep. Most of us can't help ourselves – we lose our hearts to each unsteady new lamb.

There is a price to pay. My daughter's love for Stormy made her rethink her calling as a shepherd.

Here's what happened.

Home alone one evening after a heavy snow, Bethany, now in high school, went out to do her chores. She stumbled over a newborn lamb in a snowdrift, still and close to death. She'd revived "frozen" lambs before with me. We were always amazed when a lamb that we'd taken for dead, stirred and tried to lift his head after we warmed him up. Once the lamb could raise his head, we'd feed him thawed colostrum, or first-milk, saved from last year's lambing. Within an hour, sometimes less, the lamb would be scrambling around the kitchen, his hooves drumming the linoleum as he explored his unfamiliar surroundings.

Bethany was sure she could do this.

She got right to work.

When the hairdryer wasn't having an impact, she filled the sink with very warm water, placed the lamb in a kitchen garbage bag and ruffled the plastic into an Elizabethan collar around the tiny lamb's neck before submerging it shoulder-deep in the sink. She knew to keep the water off the lamb so the newborn's distinctive scent would cling to the wool, making it more likely that her mother would still accept her – if the lamb lived.

Soon my daughter felt the little ewe lamb move. Just a little at first. Bethany added more hot water – the "lambsicle" had chilled it like an ice cube in fresh-brewed tea. By the time reinforcements arrived in the form of Bethany's dad and me, Stormy had been warmed, fed, and reunited with her mother. And Bethany had fallen for that lamb.

Stormy was beautiful. A structurally sound Oxford sheep out of stylish parents, she looked to be headed for the show ring.

Stormy was special.

Precious, loved.

Not everything ends well.

Stormy, as lambs will do, ate a few too many lamb pellets one day – probably not enough to kill her, but enough to make her pretty uncomfortable. Bethany brought her into the house and we considered the situation. Stormy grunted a little with each breath, but was on her feet and looking strong, despite her swollen belly. Bethany decided to dose her with a bloat remedy that would break up the gas bubbles. She drew up the correct amount and placed the plastic syringe in the side of Stormy's mouth and gently pushed the barrel.

At the exact moment Bethany gave the dose, Stormy took in a great deep breath in preparation to let out a protesting "BAA!"

And inhaled the oily medicine.

I grabbed the lamb and held her upside down in hopes the liquid would drain out, while Bethany frantically called the vet, who offered little hope, but reassured us that Bethany had done everything right – this was just a freak accident.

Stormy died within minutes.

I'm not sure Bethany has ever been the same. Extremely tender-hearted, she struggled every time she lost a lamb, but this – this shook her to the core. She told me she wasn't sure she could continue to raise sheep after having this – her most beloved sheep – die at her hands.

"Maybe I loved her too much," she said.

I don't think that's possible.

We love.

We love in broken and imperfect ways, but we love anyway.

Even though we know we'll lose our precious ones, we still love.

This capacity to love may be a vestige of being made in God's image; for God himself *is* love. Love is what God is – his substance, what he's made of, what he does.

He loves us more than we can possibly imagine (some of us may have trouble imagining this at all).

Nonetheless, we are precious to him.

The Psalms are full of references to God's people as being precious to him. These songs, a nation's hymnal, remind Israel that they are God's special treasure.[7] Solomon, the wisest man that ever lived, said, "He [God] will rescue the poor when they cry to him; he will help the oppressed, who have no one to defend them. He feels pity for the weak and the needy, and he will rescue them. He will redeem them from oppression and violence, for their lives are precious to him" (Psalm 72:12–14, NLT). David (who had reason to know) said, "God will never

25

walk away from his people, never desert his precious people" (Psalm 94:14, *The Message*).

My sheep are precious to me but they remain largely unaware of my love – like I remain largely unaware of the extent of God's love for me. With my brain I know that God loves me. Yes, I read it in his Word and I choose to believe it's true. But I don't often feel it or recognize it even though it flows towards me in the form of prayers offered, kindnesses done, and tiny coincidences blessing my life.

No matter what, he loves us.

Can you imagine it?

We avoid him, ignore him, disobey him, and break his heart.

His response is always and ever love.

We are precious to him.

We are the sheep of his hand.

His love has taken over our lives; God's faithful ways are eternal. Hallelujah!

PSALM 117:2, *THE MESSAGE*

Dear God,
I know that I can't comprehend your love,
but help me to catch a glimpse of it now and then.
Help me to see your love in a stranger's kindness,
feel it in the embrace of a friend,
hear it in the song on the radio.
You are there, always loving me.
Open my heart to believe that I am precious to you.

Thank you.
In the precious name of your Son, Jesus,
Amen.

Now follow...

If you have access to The Message or any newer version of the Bible, turn to Psalm 136. Read it out loud every morning this week. Hear the recurring phrase – "His love never quits" – and allow it to sink into your heart. Ask God to help you believe that it's true.

Now live like one who is loved.

27

Deadly Desires

Appetite can be deadly.

And sheep know what they like. Rich golden grain, scented of harvest. Spring-fresh fields of alfalfa, dripping with dew. Sheep are drawn to these.

And why not? The oats, corn, and wheat taste delicious and the shepherd has blended the kernels to promote healthy growth. The alfalfa, with its tasty leaves and fragrant flowers, was planted with the sheep in mind.

Why not? Why not nudge the gate open and feast on all that green? Why not knock the lid off the grain bin and feed? It's good. The shepherd got it just for them.

Why not?

Because a sheep's appetite is a dangerous thing. Patience, our elegant Cotswold ewe with the curly locks hanging over her eyes, found out the hard way. Patience didn't wait for the shepherd to measure the grain and fill the feeders. When she spotted the open door, Patience took the opportunity to jump into the granary, nudge the lid aside, and chow down.

And she gorged herself. You see, when sheep follow

their appetite, they don't know when to stop. They eat until the food runs out or they can hold no more. Indigestion in a creature with four stomachs can be fatal. Sheep depend on micro-organisms to digest their food and the populations of bacteria cannot adjust quickly to abrupt changes in diet. Without the right kinds and proportions of bacteria, food stalls in the foregut (rumen), ferments, fills the rumen with gas and produces lots of acid that the sheep's system can't handle. If the sheep has eaten too much new wet grass, the gas mixes with alfalfa bits in frothy little bubbles.

This is bloat – and it is deadly.

That's exactly what happened to my shearer's sheep. Most of her flock died right in the pasture, after a nightmare of inserting stomach tubes, dosing with oily medicines, and, after the vet arrived, piercing the sides of those still living with sharp trochars to let the deadly gas and foam escape.

29

As for Patience, we loaded her onto the pickup bed along with her lamb. The vet examined her and gave us instructions, but not much hope. He said to get her home and leave her in the pickup, since the stress of unloading would probably be too much for her. A highly ethical man, Doc Hahn only sold us enough medicine for one day, since he didn't think we'd need more than that. He assured us we could come back the next day if the ewe was still alive.

My daughter was in tears. She hadn't secured the grain bin. She knew about the dangers of bloat and the powerful drive of a sheep's cravings, but she had not experienced it firsthand. We prayed, followed the vet's instructions, then placed Patience's lamb where she could see him. While Patience groaned and fought to breathe, we fed her lamb a bottle.

Against all odds, Patience survived. I suspect she hung on for love of her lamb. Patience became a very trusting ewe, the first to come when called and very brave about injections, worming, and all manner of healthcare. Like no other sheep I've known, she had learned to trust her shepherd.

So often we get into trouble by making decisions based on our desires alone. We don't see the danger in having lunch with an attractive co-worker or buying more than we can afford. Heading in the directions of these temptations is as silly as thinking that Patience could stand in a field of sparkling, dew-drenched alfalfa and not take a bite. And then another – and another.

God knows what we are like. He knows the awfulness of our cravings.

So why doesn't he lock the granary, latch the pasture gate?

It's hard to understand why he allows us to be tempted. That doesn't stop him from testing us anyway. David, who knew a lot about being tested, wrote, "He's in charge, as always, his eyes taking everything in, his eyelids unblinking, examining Adam's unruly brood inside and out, not missing a thing. He tests the good and the bad alike" (Psalm 11:4b–5, *The Message*). David even invited God to search him and try his thoughts, finding and exposing any wickedness.

Like David (and Patience), we don't always pass the test. Even though God wants what is best for us, he doesn't force us to obey him. He wants us to choose his way, even – maybe especially – when it doesn't look best to us.

This testing that we hate has a way of changing us. Like Patience, we may grow more wise and trusting as a result. Psalm 66 says, "he... passed us like silver through refining fires, brought us into hardscrabble country, pushed us to our very limit, road tested us inside and out, took us to hell and back; finally he brought us to this well-watered place" (verses 10–12, The Message).

While I'm not a theologian and I don't understand all the ins and outs of "free will," I do know that following God would lack meaning if every alternative path were eliminated. But the alternative paths are *functionally* eliminated when we ignore them. When our focus is on the Shepherd, we'll naturally follow the path he takes, as if there were no others.

Look at him.

31

If I keep my eye on God, I won't trip over my own feet.

PSALM 25:15, *THE MESSAGE*

Why is everyone hungry for more? "More, more," they say.
"More, more."
I have God's more-than-enough,
More joy in one ordinary day
Than they get in all their shopping sprees.
At day's end I'm ready for sound sleep,
For you, God, have put my life back together.

PSALM 4:6–8, *THE MESSAGE*

Lord,
thank you that you know what we are made of
and love us anyway.
Teach us to love you and want your will.
Help us to look to you rather than to our cravings
when we decide what to pursue.
In Jesus' name, Amen.

Now follow...

This week, try to be aware of the ways you feed your hunger with appealing, but empty things. Ask God to change your heart so that you want him more than anything else.

Then spend some time with him.

What Ellie Couldn't Have

Ellie didn't mean to be destructive, but she was. We spent $2,700 to re-fence the loafing pen because of her discontent.

Ellie was in many ways a very good sheep. She gave birth to triplets and raised them unassisted (a notable accomplishment). She produced a quality fleece every year. But Ellie was just never satisfied – the hay in the feeder wasn't succulent enough and the grass in the paddock was too short. "The grass is always greener..." could have been written about her. Ellie wanted what she couldn't have.

That "better" grass was close enough – she was sure of it. She'd stick her nose through the fence, and then her head, reaching – stretching – for that enticing clump of grass. Her head fit through the fence just fine. Sheep ears, like our own, press in closer to the head when squeezing into a tight spot.

Blissfully unaware she was imprisoned, Ellie trimmed every blade of grass she could reach. When she depleted her supply, she'd back up, only then to discover she was stuck. Her ears flapped out to entrap her when she shifted into reverse.

Stuck and helpless, Ellie would begin to bleat. It got so we recognized her voice and knew her predicament as soon as we heard her. Sometimes I could get her head back through the fence with only a broken fingernail or scraped knuckle by tucking her ears back behind the cross-wires, then pushing with all my might. But Ellie never yielded ground easily – instead of cooperating, she pushed right back. Sometimes I pulled her towards me, hoping to trick the contrary ewe into moving back. That worked once or twice. When it didn't, I'd leave to search for the pliers, then clip the fence to free her.

In solving one problem, I'd created another. Pretty soon the fence had a lot more holes in it than the manufacturer intended. Even our guard dog was affected by Ellie's discontent. He found some of the holes and started to roam. He learned to hunt (not a preferred guard-dog behavior), and when we patched the holes, cutting him off from his hunting grounds, he started hunting and killing lambs instead of guarding them. We banished the beloved but disgraced guard dog - adopting him out to a non-farm family and Ellie, still unable to learn her lesson, went off to market.

We, sadder but wiser, built a new fence. The openings in this new fence are smaller than even a lamb's head. We knew that Ellie wouldn't be the last sheep to want what she couldn't have.

Asaph, a less famous psalmist than David, wrote several Psalms examining God's relationship with Israel, his sheep. In Psalm 73, Asaph marveled at those who'd gone after their own desires and ended up "at the top" – pretentious,

pampered, and overfed. He lamented, "the wicked get by with everything; they have it made, piling up riches" (verse 12, *The Message*). He couldn't figure it out.

In the sanctuary, Asaph realized that the people who looked like they were on top were headed to a bad end. Humble in God's presence, Asaph was awed that God was present to him, taking his hand, leading and blessing him.

In Psalm 74, Asaph questioned God. "You walked off and left us, and never looked back. God, how could you do that? We're your very own sheep; how can you stomp off in anger?" (verse 1, *The Message*). He begged God not to desert them despite their foolishness, and wondered if God would leave them for good.

Then Asaph considered God, rather than the rebellious behavior of his people. In verses 11 through 20, Asaph sang of the wonders of God whose way is holy. Oceans, clouds, and sky danced to his tune. Thunder and lightning and whirlwind roared as God redeemed his people.

Then, this great big God, who strode through the sea, hid himself inside his servants, who then carried out his will. Listen to how Eugene Peterson puts it in *The Message*: "Hidden in the hands of Moses and Aaron, you led your people like a flock of sheep" (Psalm 77:20).

Breathtaking to think God could work through them – and through us too, if we'll let him.

Even though God loved his people, he allowed the consequences of their behavior to follow them. He let them be defeated and didn't intervene. He cast off the rebels and chose the tribe of Judah and his servant, David, to shepherd his people.

My frustration with Ellie's willfulness, my anger at the death of the lambs, and my sorrow in making the decision to remove Ellie from the flock have given me a tiny glimpse into God's heart.

The things we do must break his heart.

Turn my heart toward your statutes and not toward selfish gain. Turn my eyes away from worthless things; preserve my life according to your word.

PSALM 119:36–37, NIV

God, I'm not trying to rule the roost. I don't want to be King of the mountain. I haven't meddled where I have no business or fantasized grandiose plans. I've kept my feet on the ground, I've cultivated a quiet heart. Like a baby content in its mother's arms, my soul is a baby content.

PSALM 131:1–2, *THE MESSAGE*

Heavenly Father,
Forgive me, please, for all the times I chase my own desires,
giving no consideration to what you might want.
Like Ellie, I can't predict the horrible consequences
of living a life based only on what I want.
Help me resist the lure of "stuff."
Draw my heart to your Word and help me know your love.
Please work through me.
In Jesus' name, Amen.

Now follow...

Meditate this week on how you regard your possessions.

Do you derive satisfaction from acquiring things?

How much is enough?

Consider the source of your contentment and your joy.

Where do you go when nothing's going right?

Try turning to God's Word when you need comfort instead of driving to the mall.

Onyx's Unbridled Passion

Crisp, fragrant breezes and russet leaves – I love fall. Fall is breeding season at our farm and I love that too. Some years we are meticulous about our work, fitting our ram with marking harnesses so we can know the due dates for each ewe. Other years, we wing it, putting the ram in and later taking him out, noting only the beginning and ending of breeding so we can be ready for the lambs. No matter which strategy we employ, I spend a lot of time watching the show.

The ewes are fertile only thirty hours every couple of weeks. The rest of the time they scatter from the ram. If none of the ewes are cycling, they'll run him ragged. He'll chase the girls, his tongue hanging out, until we take him out or someone comes into heat. When that happens, the same ewe that wanted nothing to do with him yesterday now looks coyly back over her shoulder, practically batting her eyes at him.

Now she is interested, the dance begins. The ram walks up behind her, using his sense of smell to ensure she's receptive. He curls his lip like Elvis and whispers to her before thumping her underbelly with one of his front legs, making sure she

plans to stand still for his advances. Only after this elaborate
courtship ritual does the ram consummate the union.

My husband, Mike, told me that raising sheep would
provide a good education in actions and their consequences
for our daughter. Lambing season follows breeding, year
after year. The first year we had sheep, Bethany, a fifth grader,
conducted mock weddings for J.J., the ram, and each of the
ewes. And, yes, even though we'd talked about reproduction,
raising sheep taught all of us that actions have consequences.

Every shepherd values a ram that knows his job and does
it. But Onyx, our horned purebred Rambouillet ram, showed
us the importance of boundaries. Every year in late summer,
shepherds check their fences and reinforce them, if necessary,
to make sure the rams are kept separate from the ewes until

the shepherd's chosen time. Remember, it's the shepherd that does the choosing – he may want January lambs for showing or to take advantage of the high market prices in May and June. Or maybe Spring lambs, so he can stay inside during the coldest months and put the lambs straight to pasture to minimize expenses. The shepherd, not the ram, owns the decision about lambing season, and therefore, breeding time.

No one told Onyx.

He knew there were ewes outside his pen. When the fences held against his shuddering blows, he lowered his majestic horns and blasted right through the walls of our hundred-year-old barn. We replaced the boards, but couldn't discourage his butting. Mike ended up lining Onyx's part of the barn with super-sturdy hog panels in order to prevent total demolition.

Bethany, by now in middle school and no longer conducting sheep weddings, told me that Onyx didn't know enough to wait until the right time.

Too right.

Sex, a good thing at the right time and in the right circumstances, causes harm outside the shepherd's will. Bethany signed a "True Love Waits" pledge card.

And waited.

She married last August, a wise young woman.

O God, you know how foolish I am: my sins cannot be hidden from you. Don't let those who trust in you be ashamed because of me.

PSALM 69:5–6A, NLT

Forget that I sowed wild oats; mark me with the sign of your love. Plan only the best for me, God.

PSALM 25:7, *THE MESSAGE*

Dear God,
You know me – the things I've done
and those things I've thought of doing.
Help me surrender my physical desires to your will.
Plan only your best for me.
Thank you for your love and forgiveness.
Help me to live a life that pleases you
and harms neither myself nor anyone else.
In Jesus' name, Amen.

42

Now follow...

Sex is a sensitive subject. How many times do I reassure myself by looking at the culture around me to validate the behaviors I choose rather than living according to what God says in the Bible?

Spend some time thinking about the actions you take in your personal relationships.

Now consider your thought life.

Pray about these matters this week.

Catching Emmy

Emmy dodged left, easily evading me. I had to catch her but this speedy yearling ewe didn't want to be caught. I'm glad there is no funny home video of me now – slipping in the mud when she jukes right like an NFL running back, then totally fakes me out, breaking into the open field and smirking back from the barn-door goal-line. Spike the ball – and the crowd goes wild.

In order to catch sheep, the shepherd has to understand what they like, how they act and, yes, how they think. Chasing sheep just doesn't work. Sheep are faster than people. Emmy sees the world from the perspective of a prey animal. She is suspicious, habitually unconvinced of her safety. When she is calm, she is able to make decisions. When she is afraid, she runs. Emmy, like all sheep, has a flight zone – the distance from which she estimates she could escape from a predator (a coyote, a neighborhood dog, or in this case, me). Sheep strive to maintain this distance from any approaching threat. When you enter their flight zone, they retreat.

Sheep with a big flight zone are harder to catch.

Emmy's flight zone is huge.

Still, I'm able to use what I know about sheep to catch her. Sheep move away from darkness and toward light. Darkness hides danger and light means openness and freedom. Trust me; sheep are almost impossible to catch in the open. So I know Emmy will move toward the nearest open space.

When they have a choice, sheep move against the wind rather than with it – remember most enemies of sheep hunt them by scent.

Sheep like to walk uphill rather than down.

They don't like crossing water or narrow passages or

44

slippery ground – anything that could make them an easier target for the big, bad wolf.

They hate direct eye contact too. Staring right at them is predator behavior – very wolf-like. Looking slightly off to the side, say, at the tip of their ear or their shoulder, threatens them less.

Sheep have excellent memories. When we run them through our handling equipment for worming, immunizations, or foot trimming, we'd better get everything they need done in one crack, because they'll remember the indignities they suffered the first time and be doubly difficult to round up again.

In watching my sheep, I realize how often I use similar tactics to protect myself from real or imagined threats. I remember the times I have been tricked or wounded and try to avoid situations like those that left me vulnerable. I become wary, establishing my own flight zone – one of emotional rather than physical distance. I decide how close to allow others and I move away or erect roadblocks so I'll feel safer. Like my sheep, I may wisely avoid dangerous conditions, but tend also to see threats where there are none, making choices based on fear instead of love or wisdom.

We have a Shepherd who knows us. How we are made. What's in our hearts. He knows and seeks us. The God who seeks – this Hound of Heaven – may seem scary to us, but he only wants our good. Even before we can trust him, he enters our flight zone, using his knowledge of us and his love to gather us in.

I caught Emmy by closing the pasture gates, confining

the flock to the paddock area around the barn. Walking slowly behind the entire flock, I pressured them towards the highest corner of the paddock. The group bunched up and I was able to catch Emmy because she was surrounded by all of her wooly friends. I approached from behind, taking advantage of her blind spot to grasp her under the chin and lift her head. A crook could've extended my reach, but I didn't need it this time.

Knowing Emmy was enough.

Search me, O God, and know my heart; test me and know my anxious thoughts.

PSALM 139:23, NIV

God, high above, sees far below; no matter the distance, he knows everything about us.

PSALM 138:6, THE MESSAGE

Dear Lord,
Sometimes I let my fears overpower me.
Or I cherish my wounds and decide I will never be hurt again.
I enlarge my flight zone, pushing others – maybe even you – away.
I can't imagine a vulnerable God,
one who wants a relationship with me.
Thank you for revealing your heart to me through your Son.
Thank you for knowing and accepting me just the way I am.
Now, please teach me your ways.
Today – right now – I give you my fears.
In Jesus' name, Amen.

Now follow...

Ask God to show you how you are trying to protect yourself from real or imagined harm. Pray this week about which barriers need to come down. Sit quietly before the one who knows you best and seek his wisdom.

Hold still.

Allow the Shepherd to come to you.

Cast Down

Deborah, a generous and loving ewe, found herself in trouble without warning. Heavy with lambs, she laid down to rest on uneven ground. She kept her legs under her at first, ready to get up and run if danger threatened. But as she rested, she relaxed. There was no danger. The winter sun shone down and her jet-black wool drew the heat in. She looked around, eyelids at half-mast. No threats.

Annie, the Great Pyrenees guard dog, snoozed in the sun. Deborah blinked slowly and stretched out to take an afternoon nap.

An hour passed – maybe two – and Deborah woke up. She stretched all the way down to her pointed hooves and curled her legs to bring them underneath her so she could get up.

She didn't know yet how much trouble she was in.

She just knew that she couldn't roll onto her side and over onto her legs. She gave a mighty heave, almost getting her body to forty-five degrees before hanging a moment at the tipping point; then she rolled back to her side and even further onto her back from the momentum.

Now she knew.

I doubt she knew that her predicament stemmed from lying down with her feet pointing uphill instead of down. But she knew she was stuck. Even without the weight of the lambs, she had a problem. Sheep are inherently top heavy. With the added weight of her pregnancy, her situation was hopeless. She scrabbled her feet, kicking up dust. She baaed, and in the process, ejected any remaining air from her lungs.

Her already crowded lungs.

She had carried triplets the year before and looked to be doing it again. Unusually loving, last year she'd allowed two orphan lambs to hang out with her three, sharing her warmth in the chill winter winds. Full of lambs now and ready to deliver, Deborah was almost as wide as she was long. Like a child's plastic punching bag, the ballast of her body outweighed her bony legs, rocking them to the sky after every attempt to rise.

As a shepherd would say it, Deborah was cast.

At some point, Deborah realized her situation was hopeless. When my husband pulled into the drive, he spotted her upside-down form. She might have looked comical to anyone but a shepherd. To Mike, she looked far from funny. He saw and immediately understood the seriousness of her circumstances.

Mike ran to her. With death so near, Deborah could do nothing but watch him. Completely helpless. No air to cry out, no energy to participate in her rescue.

Everything depended on the shepherd.

David had seen this situation. Every shepherd eventually

49

does. The shepherd boy probably felt the same sinking fear in his gut as he raced to the downed sheep, wondering if he'd be in time to save her.

Praying, praying.

Mike prayed too. He talked softly to Deborah as he rolled her over so her feet pointed downhill. He bent her unretracted limbs. He knelt, shouldered her onto her legs, then stood over her hindquarters and lifted her onto her feet. All very quickly.

The next part took a while. Deborah wobbled and threatened to fall back down. So Mike held her steady, applying pressure from first one side and then the other to compensate for her lack of balance.

It was cold.

Like I said, it took a while.

Finally, ever so gradually, the shepherd eased his hands off the exhausted ewe. Still unsteady, Deborah took a few steps toward the hay feeder.

Life can be like that. Everything's going fine until, suddenly, it's not. We find ourselves mired in depression. We say goodbye to a loved one, never suspecting it's for the last time. We feel fine, but the lump is cancer. We live with the illusion that we are in control. We plan our days as if we know what they'll bring. Then life takes that unexpected turn and we find ourselves incapable of coping.

Sometimes we too are cast down. Not sure how we got here so quickly and for sure unable to find our way out. David cried out to God, "Why are you cast down, O my soul?" (Psalm 42:11a, ESV).

When we are without hope, we may actually be in a

better position than when we feel strong and in charge. After all, we're not in control then either – and we bear the added disadvantage of our ignorance. When we are cast down we recognize that life doesn't depend on us. We aren't – and don't have to be – the answer to our own prayers.

God is our rock.

God is our salvation.

We depend on him.

If we are wise.

I waited patiently for the Lord to help me, and he turned to me and heard my cry. He lifted me out of the pit of despair, out of the mud and the mire. He set my feet on solid ground and steadied me as I walked along.

PSALM 40:1–2, NLT

Heavenly Father,
help me remember that I am helpless without you.
Remind me that I'm better off without even the illusion of control –
I am safest when I know I'm powerless and need to rely on you.
Thank you for being always strong to save.
Help me trust in you and not myself.
In Jesus' name, Amen.

Now follow...

Think of a time in your life when you were fully aware that

events were beyond your control. Were you afraid? Did you try to maintain control in other areas? Did you give in to despair?

Now try to remember a time in your life when you were comfortable not being in control. In my case, I remember riding home in the car at night, dressed in my pajamas, and falling asleep knowing that my parents would take care of me and I would wake up safe in my bed the next morning.

This week, meditate on the fact that even though we lack ultimate control over most of what happens to us, God is always there.

Taste — and See

In my file cabinet, under "F" for funeral, lies a snow-white lock of Cotswold wool. According to custom, shepherds are buried clasping a lock of wool so that when they get to heaven, their absences from church will be excused. I miss a fair amount of church during lambing season. That's when the shepherd's eye is most important, but since none of the ewes showed signs of imminent delivery that morning, I risked going to the early service.

When I pulled back into the drive, I saw right away that we had a problem. Lily, a yearling ewe, ran frantically in circles around the barn, baaing in distress. She looked down at the snow, turned in a tight circle, searching for something; then bolted away. She wasn't sure what she was looking for, but she acted as if she knew it was important. Too flighty and upset to be caught, her wool was streaked with the water and blood that showed she'd given birth.

Rather than wasting time trying to catch her, my daughter and I split up to search for the newborn lamb.

Nothing in the barn.

No tell-tale nest in the straw like the experienced mothers prepare by pawing the ground.

Lambing instinct is pretty variable – some new moms act as though they know just what to do, while others fail to recognize any of the feelings of labor. Birth catches them by surprise. We headed out into the snow to look for a slightly different shade of white or the depression formed by a newborn lamb at 103 degrees, melting its way into the snow.

Bethany quickly found the still-warm lamb, held it out in front of her and called Lily, who cautiously approached. We held our breath as Lily sniffed the lamb. Then, seeming almost human, she shook her head as if to say, "Nope. That's not it," before taking off to continue the search for whatever she'd lost.

We called some more and chased her, but she wasn't having any of it. Couldn't we see she was busy looking for what she'd lost? We gave up luring her with the lamb and placed it in a pen under a heat lamp, before stomping into the house to call in the reserves – Khaki, the herding dog, and Dad. The four of us proved too much for Lily. We caught her and placed her in a lambing pen with her baby.

She still ignored the lamb and struggled to jump out of the pen to continue her frenetic search. "Hang on," I said, as Mike and Bethany tried to hold and calm her. I bent down and, like scraping too much mayonnaise off a fast-food bun, slid the edge of my hand across the still-wet newborn, collecting the birthing fluid in the palm of my hand. While Bethany held the lamb below and in front of Lily, I smeared the fluid on the ewe's nose and lips.

Lily shook her head again.

Then she licked her lips – tasting. She was still for a moment; then she spoke in that magical once-a-year mommy voice. Bethany placed the lamb near Lily's mouth and she finally began to lick and dry her lamb. We backed away, marveling at the morning's events.

I know I often act like Lily. I'm afraid and know something's wrong, but I let myself get so upset I can't make sense of the situation. I feel like everything depends on me, so I run around trying to find the solution to a problem I've only dimly defined. I'm searching with all I've got, unable, like Lily, to realize that the object of my search is right beside me.

David wrote Psalm 34 about a time when he was on the run from Saul and ended up threatened by another king who didn't like him either. When death seemed certain, David got away by drooling and pretending to be insane.[8] David admitted to being anxious and afraid, and rejoiced that God heard and delivered him (verse 4). He told Israel not to hide their feelings from God. Instead, David called the people to praise God. He encouraged them to see for themselves how good God is – and run to him.

It's still advice worth taking.

Open your mouth and taste, open your eyes and see – how good God is. Blessed are you who run to him.

PSALM 34:8, *THE MESSAGE*

Dear Lord,
I know that I lose it sometimes.
I know something is wrong
but I get so upset that I can't be helped.
Calm me down. Help me remember I am not alone.
You hear my prayers and protect me.
Help me to "taste and see that you are good."
May I run to you whenever I am overwhelmed.
In Jesus' name, Amen.

Now follow...

Read Psalm 34 in a few different versions. David begins with praise and ends with promises. He says that when he turned to the Lord, God answered and delivered him from his fears. He challenges the people to seek the Lord, then tells them what to expect when they do. Consider the promises – do you want some of that?

Taste.

Try him and see.

Gates

My sheep love gates. Ever optimistic, if clueless as to what's on the other side, they rush through an opened gate as if heaven awaits them. Maybe it's because when we move the net fencing to lush, fresh pasture, my husband opens the gates with a flourish and they are rewarded immediately with toothsome forage. Even without any obvious reward, gates let something out of somewhere. They are the way out.

An open gate is freedom.

And sheep are known for wandering.

You remember my Houdini ewe, Pigeon – she doesn't wait for the gate to open. She goes where she wants to, heedless of boundaries. I've never caught her in the act of breaking out so I'm not sure if she leaps over or noses under the net. However she gets out, after a while she starts to worry about being alone (and she should be worried – I'm surprised the coyotes haven't made a meal of her). She stands at the gate then and calls until I come. Just out of my reach, Pigeon waits expectantly for me to open the gate; then walks right through without a backward glance. She knows I'll come when she calls and so far she's been lucky.

Pigeon decided to ignore the fences (again) and visit the rams last Friday. The boys, who ordinarily get along pretty well, responded by charging headlong at each other and cracking their heads together in competition over this vision of ovine loveliness who'd appeared in their midst. When I noticed the ruckus in the ram pen, I cautiously entered the ram pasture and called out to her:

"Ovi, ovi, ovi."

A good-natured escape artist, she usually comes when called.

Not Friday.

She'd start towards me, but couldn't see ahead to predict where I was leading her. I was attempting to lead her to a gate, and if she could have seen it, trust me, she'd have wanted to go through it. Unfortunately, the gate lay outside her field of vision. Pigeon followed me halfheartedly at best, and turned aside every time she was distracted by a tuft of grass, a bug, or a barn cat. I finally gave up and left her there, tempted to holler out, "Wait 'til your father gets home." Mike wouldn't have been flattered (nor Pigeon impressed).

David and the other Psalmists talked a lot about gates and it's clear that they weren't just referring to a simple pasture gate. Gates in Bible times were not merely doors or entryways, but were well-defended components of the city walls themselves. People may have worked outside the cities during the day, but they came back inside the gates to spend the night in safety. Watchmen stood guard in towers above or alongside them. Gates were places where prophets and messengers spoke, officials meted out justice, and everyone

conducted business. In Bible times, the gates of a city were often used as a metaphor for the city itself, as in Psalm 87:2–3 (NASB): "The Lord loves the gates of Zion more than all the other dwelling places of Jacob. Glorious things are spoken of you, O city of God. Selah."

63

Gates came to mean all they contained.

And in God's gates? All that he is.

Best of all, we're invited in.

Hear Psalm 100 (NLT):

Shout with joy to the Lord, all the earth!
Worship the Lord with gladness.
Come before him, singing with joy.
Acknowledge that the Lord is God!
He made us, and we are his.
We are his people, the sheep of his pasture.

Enter his gates with thanksgiving;
Go into his courts with praise.
Give thanks to him and praise his name.
For the Lord is good.
His unfailing love continues forever,
And his faithfulness continues to each generation.

People, like sheep, seem to prefer heading out of the gates toward freedom and away from restrictions. We may resist the idea of returning. One shepherd I know had to resort to a wheelbarrow to get the individuals in his flock back inside. God, too, is willing to go to extremes to bring his wandering ones home. He doesn't just invite us – he brings us back. The psalmist sings: "from my distress I called upon the Lord; The Lord answered me and set me in a large place" (Psalm 118:5, NASB).

Without God, I'm outside and at risk.

He opens the gates and draws me in.

Like Pigeon, I can follow.

Or not.

Gates wide open, arms wide open; he comes for me.

Open to me the gates of righteousness; I shall enter through them, I shall give thanks to the Lord. This is the gate of the Lord; the righteous will enter through it. I shall give thanks to You, for You have answered me, and You have become my salvation.

PSALM 118:19–21, NASB

Dear Lord,
thank you for my foolish sheep.
Thank you, too, for showing me my own foolishness.
I don't know why you love me
any more than I know why I love this silly sheep.
You do, though.
I don't have to understand it to know it's true.
Enable me to enter your gates with praise and thanksgiving,
even when – especially when – I stray.
In Jesus' name, Amen.

Now follow ...

63

God loves you and calls you to himself. He's thrown the gates open wide and calls out for you – for each of us – to come to him.

Will you?

Treats for the Sheep

Yesterday, before letting the sheep out to pasture, I looked to see if we had any day-old bread. Some of our sheep love the stuff, even more than fresh. They were in luck – two bags of half-finished hamburger and hot-dog buns languished in the bread drawer.

Two of the older ewes pricked their ears at the crackle of the bread bags as I let myself into the paddock. It had been quite a while since I'd offered them this treat, but these two hadn't forgotten.

I felt the duet of Snowdrop and Amalie bumping my hips with their noses and leaning in against my knees.

"Hang on, girls. Just a minute." I closed the gate like a ritual behind me, knowing they'd be through it like jackrabbits if I didn't.

I offered these two the bread while I watched the behavior of the rest of the flock. Most stood back and watched the two eager sheep gobble up the treat from my fingers. The rest, maybe a quarter of the group, had turned away as if to run from a threat. I knew that it was silly for them to be afraid of me, but they didn't. This is a young flock experiencing something unfamiliar. Their experience told them grain comes from a bucket and hay from the feeder. They weren't used to the idea of food coming from the shepherd's hand.

I soothed them with my voice and most of those about to bolt relaxed. Some of them turned the slightest bit back toward me. I nodded my head to them. "Good girls. You can have some too." I didn't really expect them to respond, but I could see they weren't afraid anymore. Their eyes widened. Now they were curious.

I smiled.

Some of the sheep who'd been inquisitive had watched the two old girls happily snacking and smelled the bread for themselves. They stepped a little closer. I reached over the backs of the eager eaters with the broken bread. They sniffed it; then some nibbled while others hesitated, content to observe a little longer.

Okay.

By now there were seven or eight sheep crowding around hoping for more. Once they'd gotten a taste, they were ready to stay close to me. I walked around, causing the sea of wooly creatures to shift and rearrange their positions. The curious ones let me invade their flight zone, watching closely, tensing a little in case it seemed best to run, but standing still for now. The lambs, except for Whippoorwill, all hung back. Their mamas had taught them to run from anything that scared them (and that includes just about everything – from a jacket on a fencepost flapping in the breeze to a coyote slinking along the fenceline). Just like with people, the parent's

influence shows in the child. Whippoorwill's mother trusted us, since we saved her from a dog attack last year. I wonder if she taught that to her lamb.

Could be.

Whippoorwill bobbed her head as she struggled to chew the untried food – then nosed my hand for more.

Others in the group worked their way closer to me, their backs a wooly table around me as they jockeyed for position. The closest group threatened to eat right through the bread

E SHEEP

bag, while those at the farthest edge stayed just out of reach. They stretched their necks, snuffling and even nibbling the air, coming up empty. When I reached out to give them the bread they backed away, their fear overcoming their hunger. I tried throwing them a few hunks; but they took so long checking out the goodies that by the time they'd decided to try it, another ewe had snatched it away.

I want you to know that I bring enough bread for everyone *every time* and I really want all of them to get some. I enjoy giving them goodies as much as they enjoy getting them.

But no matter how good my intentions are, some of the sheep go without. They can't quite bring themselves to trust me.

It breaks my heart.

I keep trying to win them. And I don't love them less because they don't trust me. But I long for them to be sure of me. Someday they'll need a shepherd enough to let me come close. Then they'll come to know me.

I can wait.

67

My help and glory are in God – granite-strength and safe-harbor God – so trust him absolutely, people; lay your lives on the line for him. God is a safe place to be.

PSALM 62:7–8, *THE MESSAGE*

Love God, all you saints; God takes care of all who stay close to him.

PSALM 31:23A, *THE MESSAGE*

"If you'll hold on to me for dear life," says God, "I'll get you out of trouble. I'll give you the best of care if you'll only get to know and trust me."

PSALM 91:14, *THE MESSAGE*

Dear Lord,
I say I believe in you, but sometimes I'm afraid.
I worry that if I trust you fully,
something awful will happen to me.
I want to come close and live in your love.
Take away my fear.
Help me to see you as you really are.
In Jesus' name I ask this, Amen.

68

Now follow...

Consider how much you trust your Shepherd. Are you like the comfortable old ewes, the curious uncommitted, or the out-and-out afraid? Memorize Psalm 91:14 (in any version) this week.

Remember this is God making a promise to you.

Ponder this.

And get to know and trust him.

Your Face I Seek

Facial recognition is the way we form our earliest bond, infant to parent. My sheep look at people's faces when they approach. Once they recognize the face of the shepherd, they visibly relax, their muscles softening before they turn away to the next enticing clump of grass.

I see this daily, so I wasn't surprised to find that researchers in England discovered that sheep have a sophisticated right-brain facial recognition system almost identical to ours. The humble sheep can recognize as many as fifty sheep faces and ten human faces. Once they are familiar with these ovine and human faces (and, no, sheep don't all look alike), they can remember them even after two years' absence.[9]

One of my favorite activities after a difficult day in the world is to walk out to the pasture and sit.

Just sit.

My seat, a concrete block, puts my face at eye level with the sheep. They like that, maybe because they know I'm not in a position to catch them or do anything "mean" to them. After a brief inspection, most ignore me and go about their business. A few of them, though, want to spend time with me. They walk over, nose me like a lamb, and make eye contact. Farah, one of the friendliest, stands nearby waiting for me to rub her chest or chin. She exults in this, blissing out, her eyelids at half-mast. If I continue, she lets her weight sag into her legs, as relaxed as a sheep can be while remaining upright.

This time we spend together is precious to me. I can't get into her little sheep brain to make sure, but I think it's dear to her too. We deepen our friendship; we learn to know each other in those quiet moments.

Like the sheep, we learn the face of God by spending time with him. More and more often my daily time with God begins with stopping, sitting down or kneeling, softly saying, "Here I am," and then maintaining silence. Something happens when I sit still with God – my frantic hurrying ends, all effort ceases. I imagine God enjoys this; I know that I do. Like Farah seeking me out or – if you don't have sheep – like the family dog walking over to your feet and flopping down right there, totally at ease and content to be close to you – this is what my time in God's presence feels like.

I live, exist, abide in his presence.

Here I am. In Hebrew, the word for this is *Henani*, and many men of faith used this word in response to God. Jewish scholars credit Adam with saying this first – in fact, it was the first word ever spoken. Others, notably Abraham, Jacob, Moses, and Samuel, answered, "Here I am," when God spoke to them. David said, "Oh, God, here I am, your servant, your faithful servant: set me free for your service!" (Psalm 116:16, *The Message*).

David asked God to "Let your face shine on your servant; save me in your unfailing love" (Psalm 31:16, NIV). David, who God commended as one "whose heart beats to my heart,"[10] knew God's love. Over and over David sought God's face. He begged him not to turn away from him, or hide his face from him.

Our desire for God's face is miniscule compared to his desire for ours. Hard to imagine that he loves us that much. My feelings for Farah suggest that he does. We, small creatures lost in a very large landscape, can, at a moment's notice, get face-time with the maker of it all.

Selah.

As for me, I will behold thy face in righteousness: I shall be satisfied, when I awake, with thy likeness.

PSALM 17:15, KJV

Seek the Lord, and his strength: seek his face evermore.

PSALM 105:4, KJV

Lord,
I seek so much that isn't you.
When the choice is left to me,
I find other ways to use my time.
I don't mean to ignore you,
but I let myself be distracted.
If you get any time at all, it's tired time.
I am most myself when I am right with you.
Don't give up on me.
Don't hide your face from me.
Here I am.
Amen.

72

Now follow...

Spending time with God doesn't have to be hard. Prayer, quiet time – these may work for you or you may struggle with guilt because they don't. Try sitting in silence for a period of time every day. Think of yourself as sitting in the presence of God. You will be.

Baby Talk

Every year, when ice and snow coat the ground or when they merge with the soil to make mud, I am privileged to overhear the sheep speaking to their lambs. For most of the year, the ewes make a sound like a small-scale foghorn: "Baa."

Pretty generic.

That nursery-rhyme sound is not what I'm talking about. The voice of the ewe who has just given birth is something totally different. If a sheep could whisper, that would be the sound. Instead they murmur softly to their lambs – *mr-er-er-er* – as they dry the babies' soaking wet wool. Each mama sounds a little bit different when she does this, but every one of them sounds enchanting. Within a few hours, the lambs (twins are most common) consistently answer their mother.

She speaks.

They answer.

The ewes speak patiently and repeatedly to their little ones during the first few days of life.

After getting to know each other during a few days in the lambing jug (the shepherds' word for a small pen), we place several mothers and their lambs together in a larger mixing pen. Here the lambs are put to their first test. The mothers call the lambs and the lambs have to locate their mothers. Positive and negative consequences ensue – if lambs approach a ewe who isn't their mother, she butts them away, usually gently but sometimes with a lot of force. When the lambs find their own mothers, they're rewarded with warm milk and still more love talk. We stay nearby to make sure the lambs figure out the rules and to identify rough ewes for culling.

After a few days in the mixing pen, when the lambs know their mothers' voices and come running when they're called, the moms and babies graduate to the paddock. We still keep a close eye on the group to make sure the families stay within hearing distance. A few lambs invariably get lost and have to be caught and reunited, but for the most part the little lambs keep their ears tuned to the unique voices of their mamas while ignoring the rest of the barnyard cacophony.

We also observe the mothers' attentiveness to the lambs' voices. Lost lambs, like children of any species, cry. By now, the mothers know their children's voices and answer them. Some give only a perfunctory answer though, while others call out repeatedly and urgently so the errant lambs can home in on the signal and find their way back. The best mothers combine their voices with action – if the lambs don't find them in a reasonable amount of time (the older the lamb, the longer the interval), the mothers set out in search of them, calling their names as they go. There's joy at each reunion as lamb tails wag and the relieved ewe sniffs her babies, making sure they're her own.

God speaks to us in a still, small voice and claims us. Like the lambs, we can learn to recognize his voice by listening to him. Like my strongest mothers, he calls out to us, his little ones, and looks for us to come. Best of all, even if we ignore him and go our own way, he seeks us.

He loves us with a love that is different and better than any kind of love we can imagine. But he lets us glimpse it here.

Here, in a muddy pasture, love abounds.

Incline your ears to the words of my mouth.

PSALM 78:1B, NASB

I hear this most gentle whisper from One I never guessed would speak to me.

PSALM 81:5B, *THE MESSAGE*

Should I wander off like a lost sheep – seek me! I'll recognize the sound of your voice.

PSALM 119:176, *THE MESSAGE*

Dear God,
The "little" love we experience here is so beautiful –
how can I begin to comprehend your perfect love for me?
It's hard to believe you speak to me.
Or want me near you.
Help me to believe it's true.
Help me to listen and learn to hear you,
recognizing your voice in the chaos of my life.
In Jesus' name, Amen.

76

Now follow...

When you read your Bible this week, pay special attention to times when God speaks. Psalm 50:7–15 is a good place to start. So is Psalm 81. Pay attention to how God sounds in the Word when he's pleased, disappointed, or angry.

Now think about the times when you felt "nudged" to do something – call or visit a friend, smile at a stranger. Could that have been God speaking to you without words?

Pay attention – incline your ear – and ask God to guide you.

David knew God's voice; you can learn to discern it too.

Constant Care

The eye of the shepherd fattens the lamb.

ANONYMOUS

We ordered a closed-circuit camera for the barn last night. For many years during lambing season we have set our alarm clocks to go off every two hours, taking turns getting dressed, booting up (for real, not on a computer), and slogging through snow, ice, or mud to check on the ewes. My friends ask me why I would put myself through this. The answer is simple – it needs to be done.

Pregnant ewes can show signs that they will give birth soon, but I've learned not to count on it. If I think a particular ewe is close to delivering, I confine her to a lambing pen overnight, but that doesn't relieve me of my responsibility to keep her and her babies safe. If a ewe labors more than an hour without giving birth, she needs an internal exam to determine which part of the lamb is coming out first. One leg forward, tangled twins – there are a lot of variations. If the shepherd isn't watching and ready to intervene, mother and babies may die.

Why two hours, you may ask? Well, it's cold in Central Illinois. In our most frigid lambing season, the mercury hit 26 below zero, freezing an umbilical cord at the 45-degree angle that was formed when the lamb hit the ground. If a lamb is born right after a barn check, it too could be frozen before the next one.

This happens more often than you might think.

Most of the ewes are shy and when the shepherd disturbs them, labor stops for a time. So, even if everything looks just fine when you shine your flashlight around the barn, you can still find a frozen lamb (or two) at the next barn check. Lambs are soaking wet when they're born. I've found them still on their feet but encased in a thin coat of ice that cracks like an eggshell when I pick them up. If they're alive when I get to them, they usually survive. So, even though lambing season leaves me as tired as a mom with a new young'un, two hours it is.

Lambing season requires the most intense observation, but sheep at any age and any stage benefit from the shepherd's watchful eye. Lambs touch the electric net fencing, panic when they receive a shock and get caught in it. Ewes get cast or get their heads stuck in a bucket. (Don't laugh. Well, okay. It is pretty funny.) A sheep in this situation baas in distress, her voice echoing back at her; she runs aimlessly, unable to see where she's going. If you don't catch this early, your sheep can charge right through the fence and head for the hills – or the road. I admit to laughing while I rescue them. And I try to remember not to leave empty buckets around.

Then there are the predators. Our place teems with coyotes. Sometimes I try to count their voices when they sing at night or giggle after a successful hunt. I never succeed at it – all I know is there's a lot of them. They're bold, too – coming within a foot of the fence during lambing, when the air is rife with blood-scent. Annie and Cooper, our Great Pyrenees guard dogs, ensure our flock's survival, patrolling the perimeter all night long.

In David's time, the shepherd lived with the flock twenty-four hours a day. Today, sheep don't provide even a subsistence income, so every shepherd I know has another source of income. Mike and I both work away from the farm. I rely on dogs and fences to keep the sheep safe.

To David's sheep, *he* was safety. No fences then. The shepherd's presence, his eye, protected them. His courage and his strong arm dealt with those who would harm them. If he used a fold – an incomplete circular enclosure of stone or hedges where sheep were penned for the night – he slept in the doorway. In effect, he was the doorway between the sheep and a host of dangers in the world.

Even though I am unable to provide 24/7 watch over my flock, the camera will help me approach that. I lose a few sheep – lambs and ewes – every year because I am not able to provide the constant care they require.

Like most people today, I like to think of myself as independent and capable. When I was a teenager I couldn't wait to be grown-up and able to take care of myself. I don't like to admit that my self-sufficiency is mostly an illusion. Things happen – illness, accidents. Sometimes my own foolishness leaves me lost, running aimlessly, but all I hear are my own cries for help coming back at me.

I'm often helpless.

Thank God I'm cared for.

Don't get me wrong. I can and should do all that I can to live responsibly. Being cared for is not an excuse for laziness, selfishness, or stupidity. I just recognize that much of what happens to me is beyond my control. And I want to recognize my need for a shepherd, someone to watch over me.

Sheep need unceasing oversight. Humbled, I admit that I do too.

God watches.

He watches me.

You are with me.

Psalm 23:4b, NKJV

God keeps an eye on his friends, his ears pick up every moan and groan.

Psalm 34:15, THE MESSAGE

The one who watches over you will not slumber. Indeed, he who watches over Israel never slumbers or sleeps. The

Lord himself watches over you! The Lord stands beside you as your protective shade. The sun will not harm you by day, nor the moon at night. The Lord keeps you from all harm and watches over your life. The Lord keeps watch over you as you come and go, both now and forever.

PSALM 121:3B–8, NLT

Heavenly Father,
Free me from the illusion that I am in control.
Thank you for watching over me.
Thank you for your unceasing care.
When I feel alone and afraid, reassure me of your love.
In Jesus' name, Amen.

81

Now follow...

This week, ask God to show you the ways in which he cares for you. Keep a list, if you like. Notice things like your safe trip home from work, your plane touching down safely, a good night's sleep. If things are falling apart and going wrong left and right, ask God to reveal one way he is caring for you.

Listen for his answer.

Misread

Rudi was in trouble. She was lambing for the first time and making no progress. Her rapid breathing raised puffs of mist in the cold air. She didn't know what was happening to her – not like the older sheep who had lambed before. What's more, she'd been pushing way too long when I found her. The whites of her eyes signaled fear.

My heart went out to her. Confused and exhausted, she heaved herself up and ran out of my reach as soon as I approached.

"Come, sheep," I called softly. But she would not.

I ended up catching her with my crook. She struggled, but I was ready for that. I turned her head back towards her shoulder, making her lose her balance and lean into my legs. This is the way to lay a sheep down without hurting her. I hurried to kneel down, throwing a leg over her wooly back to restrain her. She moaned and fought when I untangled the unborn lambs, then eased them onto the straw. Steam rose from the twins as the ewe reached out to clean and claim her babies.

How like that frightened ewe we often are. She needed

help and would die without it, but she ran from the one who could save her. I wanted only her good, but the help I provided didn't seem very good to her. She hated the yank of the crook around her neck. She didn't understand why I bent her head to the side and threw her off-balance. When she wanted to get up, I dug my knee into her side, frustrating her frantic efforts. I was her only hope, but she never understood my heart. She couldn't know that I love her and would do anything in my power to save her.

83

Like my ewe, we often look at circumstances and quake in fear. We don't understand what is happening to us. We ask God for help, but it seems like things are only getting worse. Our coping mechanisms fail us; we're knocked off-balance and fall. We are afraid and we cry out, but new pain grips us. We wonder who will help us, even while the Savior holds us tightly, working in that moment for our good.

Was I angry with my little ewe when she resisted me? Never.

If she had trusted me, it would have been much easier to help her. But concern and love were all I felt. Jesus wants us to rely on him. He is the Good Shepherd and is more worthy of trust than any human shepherd.

We can always be sure of his love.

As a father has compassion on his children, so the Lord
has compassion on those who fear him; for he knows how
we are formed, he remembers that we are dust.

PSALM 103:13–14, NIV

Heavenly Father,
help us to trust you and the way you work in our lives.
Thank you for being a very present help in trouble.
Amen.

Now follow...

Trying to learn about God is good. But God's goodness toward
us doesn't depend on our understanding of the situation. God
is too great for us to comprehend.

My sheep don't have to understand me to trust me.

Tell God you trust him.

Reflect on his response.

Rest

From my kitchen window, I watch the rhythm of the sheep.

The pastures are Crayola® green. The sun is warm, but not hot. The sheep repeat a ceaseless cycle of work and rest, work and rest. They graze, catching the blades of grass between their lower incisors and the pad of their upper gums. Because of that unique tooth-to-gums interface, they squeak as they crop the grass. Grazing doesn't cause much exertion. They're basically just standing around eating. Nonetheless, after a while, as if hearing a silent signal, they return to the shade of the barn and choose places to lie down.

On a nice day like this, they might doze, eyelids sagging. Then, after an hour or so of stillness, they're up again, heading out to pasture.

Work and rest.

Work and rest.

Maybe they're on to something.

Like so many people, I live an overcommitted life. I am *so* busy. Sometimes I'm almost proud of that, as if having my fingers in so many pies makes me important or indispensable.

I'm not really sure about the effectiveness of all this activity
on my part. I don't really have the time to give it much
thought. I try frantically to stay on task, to get it all done and,
despite all my hard work, feel somehow frustrated at how
much I don't accomplish.

I'm not alone in this. Our culture holds busyness in high
regard – "If you want something done, ask a busy person to do
it."[11] We organize our days, our hours and minutes, spending
ourselves into exhaustion.

My sheep don't do that.

Well, yeah, I admit they don't have much on their
agenda. And if they saw a to-do list, they'd probably eat it.
Still, they know how to rest. And they actually do it.

God does not intend for us to live at a constant frantic
pace. He knows we need rest. He designed the need for sleep
into our makeup and set up the Sabbath for our benefit.
Solomon, wisest of all, said, "It is useless for you to work

so hard, from early morning until late at night, anxiously working for food to eat; for God gives rest to his loved ones" (Psalm 127:2, NLTse).

Rest restores. David knew this well. The Lord, his shepherd, *made* him lie down in green pastures and restored his soul (emphasis mine). Read Psalm 23 slowly, as if you'd never seen it before.

> God, my shepherd! I don't need a thing.
> You have bedded me down in lush meadows,
> you find me quiet pools to drink from.
> True to your word, you let me catch my breath
> and send me in the right direction.
> Even when the way goes through Death Valley,
> I'm not afraid when you walk by my side.
> Your trusty shepherd's crook makes me feel secure.
> You serve me a six-course dinner right in front of my
> enemies.
> You revive my drooping head; my cup brims with
> blessing.
> Your beauty and love chase after me every day of my life.
> I'm back home in the house of God for the rest of my life.

THE MESSAGE

Yes, the idea of resting appeals to us, but the practice eludes us. We are obligated to so many things. We have no time to waste. We multitask and are proud of it – our minds leaping ahead to the next item on our list before we've finished the last.

Stop. Be still.

87

This is an important message from God. He really wants us to get it, so he uses repetition to get his point across: "Be still, and know that I am God" (Psalm 46:10, KJV); "Commune with your own heart upon your bed, and be still" (Psalm 4:4, KJV); "Quiet down before God, be prayerful before him" (Psalm 37:7a, *The Message*); and so many more.

Stillness offers our best hope of knowing God. Being still before him, paying attention as we sit before him in silence – this is what God wants – what he tells us to do. He wants our attention.

Why? I find myself asking.

I want to get to the bottom line. Why does he want this?

Underneath it all, I think I'm afraid that God wants my attention so that he can tell me what to do. And I'm not sure I want him to tell me what to do – maybe because I have so much to do already that I can't handle it if he does.

Here's a thought.

Maybe God doesn't want our attention to tell us to do something.

Maybe he just wants our attention.

My sheep balance work and rest.

So can I.

Step out of the traffic! Take a long, loving look at me, your High God, above politics, above everything.

PSALM 46:10, THE MESSAGE

Relax and rest. God has showered you with blessings.

Let all that I am wait quietly before God.

PSALM 62:5, NLTsE

Heavenly Father,
help me to slow down.
Teach me to rest in your presence.
To abide.
This seems very hard to me –
even harder than some arduous task.
I do want to know you.
Show me the way.
In Jesus' name, Amen.

89

Now follow...

This week, experiment with resting. Take a nap. Sit on the porch swing. Go to bed an hour earlier. Find out what happens if you spend an entire day without working. Try setting aside some time every day to sit quietly with God. Get comfortable and be still (the New American Standard Version renders that phrase as "cease striving"). If it helps, you can set a timer – five minutes is a good place to start. By the end of the week you may want to choose a longer time.

Notice.

Pay attention.

Relax.

Hands-on Love

Every year we have a few lambs who are, shall we say... slow.

These little lambs just can't figure out how to survive. Maybe their births were difficult and their brains were deprived of oxygen. For whatever reason, these forlorn little creatures don't latch onto their mamas' teats.

This is an emergency.

Colostrum is produced early in lactation and is a miraculous substance, full of antibodies against infection, anti-inflammatory cells, and quick energy. The lambs are ready to receive the milk, with microscopic channels in their digestive systems only temporarily open to these immune factors. Scientists aren't sure how quickly these channels close in any individual lamb, but their advice is clear: lambs need to eat within an hour of birth – half an hour is even better.

Even our smartest lambs couldn't possibly understand this – they operate on instinct. But instinct has failed these obtuse little ovines who can't even manage to suckle. They don't know what to do.

But the shepherd does.

My husband and I take turns watching the new arrivals with one eye on the clock. At half an hour, we intervene. We tap the lamb above its tail, pushing it in the right direction. We push the teat toward the baby's mouth and, if that isn't enough, we pry the lamb's mouth open and place the nipple inside. We tickle the lamb's tail, trying all sorts of tricks to get the lamb started. All this, mind you, while lying under a nervous mom in not-so-clean straw or pressing her against the wall with our heads while maneuvering the lamb and the faucet.

When our tricks fail, we feed some of last year's colostrum, harvested from a ewe with a single lamb and frozen for just such circumstances. If the lamb is strong enough to hold her head up, we offer a bottle. If the lamb is too weak, I slide in a feeding tube, checking carefully that the tip is in the stomach and not the lungs before allowing gravity to send the first milk into the lamb.

Sometimes just this one feeding does the trick. We watch to see if the lamb actively looks for the teat and eats on its own. If not, we make the trip to the barn every few hours to hold the ewe still and crawl under her to help the baby again.

And again.

However long it takes.

Our record is four days.

We were as tired as new parents when that lamb finally figured things out.

I have to point out that this kind of intervention doesn't go on in the large flocks in the western United States or in the even larger flocks in Australia and New Zealand. I imagine, though, that David as a young shepherd boy may have tended his flock much like we do. Our little operation is small enough that each loss affects us more financially (and certainly emotionally) than shepherds of larger flocks. Because we keep a small flock, we know our sheep and have cried when we watch any ewe mourn her lost little one. We are willing to be inconvenienced for the sake of one lamb.

And, yes, we love them.

That love requires us to literally "get down and dirty" with them.

Love always does.

But you, O God, are both tender and kind, not easily angered, immense in love, and you never, never quit. So look me in the eye and show kindness, give your servant the strength to go on, save your dear, dear child!

PSALM 86:15–16, THE MESSAGE

Dear Heavenly Father,
thank you for your hands-on love.
Help me to recognize your hands
as they nudge me in the right direction.
Thank you for your patience with me
and your love that I cannot understand.
I'm so glad I'm yours.
In Jesus' name,
Amen.

Now follow...

A lot of what I do as a Christian is directed towards understanding God and learning about him. Lately I'm wondering if I'm a little off target there. Understanding isn't the same as knowing – being in relationship with – someone. A psychiatrist may seek to understand someone, but isn't looking for friendship.

This week consider the difference between knowing about someone, even being an expert on him, and *knowing him* – truly being his friend. My sheep can't hope to understand me any more than I can hope to understand God. But my sheep know me.

And you can know God. In fact, he is making every effort, using all his tricks, to draw you to himself.

Ask God to open your eyes and show you how to get to know him better.

Ruminating

Sheep do this amazing thing. They ruminate.

"What's that?" you might say.

Ruminating is re-chewing.

I can hear you thinking, Why is this important to me (or anyone, for that matter)?

Stay with me – there's something here.

As you've heard me say before, a sheep is a creature with many stomachs (four, to be exact). The first of these stomachs is the rumen. It's sort of a holding pen for all the grass, hay or grain the sheep have recently managed to eat. Sheep graze opportunistically. When they're brought into good pasture, they tear grass off the ground in large clumps. They don't take the time then to thoroughly chew it. They swallow the first mouthful and then they reach for more. If their lambs cry out to them, the ewes answer, their baaing like a child talking through a mouthful of marshmallow, but they don't interrupt their grazing.

Well-fed sheep may look relaxed when they graze, but, probably because of their vulnerability to predators, they still consume their meals all at once. If people ate like sheep, we would sit at the table feeding ourselves by placing the fork in our mouths over and over again and repeatedly swallowing without taking any time to chew. When food is abundant and available, sheep work hard to take it in.

Later, their hunger satisfied, the sheep withdraw from the pasture into the safer paddock. Now they rest. If they sense no threats, they subject the stored grass to further processing by forcefully expelling air in a small burp or cough, moving the grass from the rumen back to the mouth. Then they contentedly chew the food they ate earlier. Relaxed sheep contentedly chewing their cud – this may have been the most common sight in Bible times. Ruminating sheep probably looked thoughtful; lying around masticating, eyelids at half-mast. Thoughtful enough, at least, for the word "ruminate" to come to mean meditate, reflect, ponder.

David grew up watching sheep do this. When he thought about God, he realized he'd taken on a concept far beyond his understanding. But, as a shepherd, he had a lot of time on his hands. Time for contemplation, time to turn his thoughts over and over in his head. He wrote poems and sang songs about the wonder of God.

> I remember the days of old;
> I meditate on all Your doings;
> I muse on the work of Your hands.
> I stretch out my hands to You;
> My soul *longs* for You, as a parched land.
> Selah.

PSALM 143:5–6, NASB (EMPHASIS MINE)

David was fond of inserting pauses for thought in his psalms, wisely recognizing the richness and complexity of these ideas. In order to slow the listener down, he asked them to pause for a while and think on those ideas – maybe playing a musical interlude to provide the time for reflection. Since the concepts were too complex to be digested in quick unthinking gulps, he offered his listeners something to think about and used the word "Selah" to indicate a hiatus to allow insight to grow.

Contemplation may seem out of place in our hurry-up world. The frenetic pace of my other job, full of technology and tension, dissolves when I walk through the pasture gate. For Madeleine L'Engle fans, I leave *chronos* (this world's clock time) and enter *kairos* (God's timelessness) when I'm present with my sheep.

Shepherding, looking to one's flock, lends itself to thought. You may enter that timeless state when you go fishing, or knit, or run. You don't have to have a flock of woolies in the back yard in order to practice contemplation. You just need to get quiet and alone. My sheep have taught me the importance of not only taking in *but also* later pondering what I heard in Sunday's sermon or read in a thought-provoking Christian book. I allow myself to think, slowly and at leisure, about what these truths mean and how they apply to me where I am right now.

In our instant world of fast food, microwaves, and seemingly all knowledge available at the click of a mouse, we need to slow down. The knowledge of God and his ways isn't and can't be instant.

Ruminate.

Absorb all that he has for you.

Remember,

it takes time.

Selah.

You thrill to God's word, you chew on scripture day and night.

PSALM 1:2B, *THE MESSAGE*

I'm chewing on the morsel of a proverb; I'll let you in on the sweet old truths.

PSALM 78:2, *THE MESSAGE*

Your words are so choice, so tasty; I prefer them to the

best home cooking. With your instruction, I understand
life.

PSALM 119:103–104A, THE MESSAGE

Heavenly Father,
Help me to read your Word for all it's worth.
Bring it to my mind over and over again.
Feed me with your wisdom as I think about your Word.
Even when I don't understand it,
let the juices nourish my heart as I meditate on your love.
In Jesus' name I ask this, Amen.

Now follow...

Try picturing a scene in the Bible. Imagine yourself as one of
the people in the story. What would you see, hear, even smell
if you were there? Imagine that you are watching the speaker
say the words that are on the page in front of you.

Or, try focusing on a word that stands out to you in the
passage. Read the passage slowly and out loud, letting the
sounds fall on your ears.

Let yourself wonder.

Earmarked

For many years our sheep went on the road every summer. The fair circuit is an education in itself, whether it's just the county 4-H Fair or the series of county fairs and one or two state fairs thrown in for good measure. The sheep don't give it much thought (they don't have to take anything along), but the shepherds practically empty the barn. Trunks full of show clothes, wool outfits (in July!) for the Shepherds' Lead competition (a sort of sheep-on-a-leash fashion show), combs and clippers, soap and harnesses, refrigerators and sleeping bags – you get the idea. It's a lot of work and a lot of fun, too.

Sheep are shampooed, blown-dry, and trimmed to present their best features. Judges squint at the animals while fresh-faced beauty queens adjust their tiaras after brushing the dust off their jeans. A lot goes on in the sheep barn, and lest you think this is quaint and just for fun, a winning animal in some categories takes home hundreds of dollars in prize money and thousands of dollars in auction revenue. Some years, shepherds are caught cheating by feeding or introducing forbidden substances. Sometimes the cheating took place months before "behind the barn," when sheep were secretly crossbred or birthdates were adjusted to give the shepherd an edge.

Still and overall, shepherds are an honest bunch. They help competitors show their sheep and work as one to catch any sheep that break free and threaten to venture out of the show barn.

One of our nights at the state fairgrounds, an anonymous sheep leaned against the gate to her pen – and it opened. She was in an unfamiliar place and was probably curious. Maybe she was trying to find her own barn. The lights were out and the shepherds lay stretched out on their cots or curled in their sleeping bags. Some were home in bed. No one heard the ewe lamb at first. Her hooves tapped against the concrete, but softly, softly. Until she sniffed a snoozing shepherd, no one realized she was out.

Surprised to find herself nose to nose with someone else's sheep, my daughter quickly oriented herself and caught the fleecy fugitive. We closed her in an empty pen and walked quietly through the dimly-lit barn trying to figure out where she'd come from. A few sheep began to stir and baa (when they saw us moving around, they thought it was morning, and therefore that breakfast, would be forthcoming). Rather than let them all wake up and get rowdy, we snuck back to bed. The wanderer was safe for now and like all of the sheep in the barn, she sported an eartag. We may not have known whose sheep she was, but when the sun came up and the fair officials arrived, her eartag would tell us who she was and get her back where she belonged.

And it did.

Sheep are marked with their shepherd's name. Farm names and numbers on a little piece of plastic tell us whose sheep these are. Before plastic eartags, shepherds marked their sheep by notching their ears in distinct patterns. The technology is ever changing, with tiny computer chips able to track livestock movement and identify their source. Regardless of the technique, members of a flock are identified as belonging to someone.

Are we?

Can anyone tell whose we are?

How can they?

Some Christ-followers wear crosses around their necks, but that can be as much style as statement – many who wear crosses aren't Christians. T-shirts and casual wear ride the racks at the Christian bookstore, so I guess that's another possibility.

In Psalm 25, David asks God to mark him with the sign of his love.[12] This reminds me of Jesus telling his followers, "By this shall all men know that you are My disciples, if you have love one to another" (John 13:35, KJV).

This love – this is our earmark. God, who *is* love, loves us. Because we are loved, we can afford to extend love to others. And when we do, people are drawn to the source of that love.

He loves us.

We love him, then others.

Others see him too.

103

We're depending on God; he's everything we need.
What's more, our hearts brim with joy since we've taken
for our own his holy name. Love us, God, with all you've
got – that's what we're depending on.

PSALM 33:20–22, *THE MESSAGE*

God, mark us with grace and blessing! Smile! The whole
country will see how you work.

PSALM 67:1–2, *THE MESSAGE*

Dear God,
Sometimes I wonder if anyone can tell I'm your follower.
Does my life look any different
from the lives of everyone around me?
I want you to be visible in my life.
Thank you for pouring out your love on me.
Guide my relationships so I live out your love,
aware, yes, that others may see me;
but wanting my actions to please only you.
In Jesus' name, Amen.

104

Now follow...

Sit in the sun, if the season allows, or maybe a sunny window. Imagine those warming rays to be God's love. Absorb it. Feel it. Now imagine a force infinitely greater. God, who is love, shines on you.

Now, lightly, easily, as if you are playing a game, radiate compassion, kindness, and concern to others as you go about your day.

God's love will be evident in a dark world.

It'll leave a mark.

Led, Not Driven

Every so often Mike and I need to do some hands-on healthcare maintenance for the flock. In order to do this with the least amount of wear and tear on them (and ourselves), we herd them into a livestock handling system that crowds them all together then arranges them single-file in a chute where we can give them vaccinations and worm medicine or whatever their need of the moment is. The sheep don't really enjoy the care we give them in the chute and would prefer not to go in the direction of the handling pen.

The easiest way to get your sheep where you need them, the method most in harmony with their nature, is to lead them. Since they dislike the handling equipment, we offer the added incentive of grain, carried high in a bucket where all the sheep can see it. We shake or tap the pail so they hear the grain whisper, shifting against itself, while its fragrance wafts a promise of full tummies and satisfied cravings. Tempting them through several of their senses usually works (for me, too, unfortunately).

We are working now on a program of intermittent

rewards to improve the flock's attitude towards the equipment itself. We lead the sheep to the equipment, run them quickly through it without doing anything unpleasant to them, then offer the grain as payoff for their cooperation.

Whether or not a reward is in the offing, sheep, like people, enjoy being led and resist being driven. Sometimes (usually when we're out of grain) the sheep spook and scatter just before entering the pen. Now we're in the soup – they're wise to us and wary. They know we want them in the pen and they suspect they'll get nasty medicines given with sharp needles or metal tubes. We can't reason with them or attempt to convince them their unpleasant experiences in the chute are a good thing. That's *waaay* beyond them. Since leading sheep requires their consent (and that's lacking), we're forced to resort to driving.

The sheep hate being driven – they might respond to it, but they hate it. We use our herding dog, a Cardigan Welsh Corgi, to drive the sheep. She barks, runs at the sheep and compels them to go where she wants. Sheep feel stressed when they are pushed and manipulated by threats. No joy – no relationship here. Only force. Might makes right. They don't like it. We don't either.

I found a story on the internet about Middle Eastern shepherds. A tour group visiting the region observed a man driving his sheep from behind. Their guide recognized this as unusual. He called out, "How is it that you are driving these sheep? I have always been told that the shepherd here leads his sheep."

The man replied, "The shepherd does lead his sheep.

The butcher drives and I am the butcher!"[13]

God, the Great Shepherd, prefers to lead his people. When we refuse to be led, he, motivated by love, may choose to drive us at times. But when his people willingly follow, God doesn't resort to driving.

Stressed, unable to think it through, we may assume that it's God nipping at our heels. I suspect that most of the time, the one driving us is not our Shepherd, but the enemy. We may be driven by our fears, our quest for perfection, or our society's expectations. As Stasi Eldridge said so well, "We long for intimacy… but the message we hear – whether from a driven culture or a driven church – is *try harder*."[14]

THE SHEEP OF HIS HAND

Christians may be the most driven segment of our society. We struggle with sin and wonder why. We buy books that tell us how to live victoriously – just follow this simple formula. We know the world is watching us and we try oh-so-hard to be good, and when we fail, we break out the masks and fake it, thinking that God's reputation will be tarnished if we don't.

And the enemy laughs.

I have to admit that much of the time I live as a driven Christian. I think I know what I'm supposed to do and how I'm supposed to live; so I grit my teeth and attempt to do it. I'm more aware than I should be of others' eyes on me. I use the imagined opinions of other people as a mirror and a motivation for the actions I take.

I might read an article in a Christian magazine – usually one with a list of steps to take – and I measure myself against it and come up short. I determine to do better and turn to my own methods to achieve that goal. If I did remember to read my Bible, then you can bet I slipped in some other area. When I shore that up, I find another flaw to work on. Pretty soon I'm tangled in my own efforts, eyes firmly on myself, my effort, my failures, my strengths.

I'm driven.

I'm trying to "get it right."

To be perfect, above reproach.

It never works.

I have to admit, I'm tired of being driven. Tired of trying so hard and failing so often. Any natural gifts and talents I have only delay the realization that I am insufficient – I can't do this alone.

You'd think I'd get wise to this. If any of us could please God with our efforts, why would we need a Savior?

If God doesn't need our efforts, what does he need?

He needs our consent,

    our willingness,

        our trust,

            our *yes*.

Driving myself (or allowing myself to be driven) will never be the secret of the Christian walk.

Like sheep, we are designed to be led.

That's right, led.

Sheep don't bear burdens, do tricks, or achieve greatness. They live with their shepherd, eat from his hand, and effortlessly, without even noticing it, grow wool to meet his needs.

They are used by the shepherd when they allow themselves to be led.

    Not driven.

109

Going through the motions doesn't please you, a flawless performance is nothing to you.

PSALM 51:16, *THE MESSAGE*

Teach me how to live to please you, because you're my God. Lead me by your blessed Spirit into cleared and level pastureland.

PSALM 143:10, *THE MESSAGE*

Dear God,
I don't know why I try to live the Christian life
as if it is a set of rules to keep.
I'm sorry.
Lead me by your Spirit, because you are my God.
In Jesus' name, Amen.

Now follow...

Jesus, as always, is our example – our Shepherd to follow. When people wondered at the things they saw Jesus do, he said that he did nothing of himself, only what he saw the Father doing (John 5:19).

110

This, then, is our assignment this week. Choose one of the Gospel books – Matthew, Mark, Luke, or John – it doesn't matter which one. Read it, focusing on what you see Jesus doing. Think about his actions, look for patterns, and pray for wisdom. Then ask God to lead you. You, personally, in your life situation.

He will.

What to Expect When Your Mom is a Bucket

Their mother died because of a ruptured uterine ligament. Heavy with twins, Madeleine, my old but still productive ewe, had exited the barn with her belly hanging ominously low, only just skirting the snow. We rushed her to the vet, who saved the twins, but not their mother.

We bottle-fed those little orphans for almost two months, long past the time most prudent shepherds would bear the cost of milk replacer. Daily we filled a big square bucket with latex nipples mounted on three of its sides. The twins came running when we thumped the bucket and hung it on their pen.

When we tried to retire the bucket, offering a single bottle for each at bedtime, they seemed unusually hungry. The lamb boys raced to the fence and sucked so fiercely that they didn't even stop to breathe.

"Maybe they're thirsty," Bethany said. "Have you ever seen them drinking?"

I thought back. I couldn't remember seeing them at the water tank but I hadn't been paying that much attention.

So, we watched the boys. Bethany was right – they never went anywhere near the tank.

The other lambs walked up to the water right alongside their mamas. They touched their lips to the surface of the water and drank. Nothing to it.

But not the lost boys.

They didn't know how.

Although I had provided them with nourishment, I hadn't provided them with mothering. Raising lambs is so much more than giving them a bottle. Our orphans had no model, no example to follow – no one to guide their steps. And this caused no end of problems.

Imagine my surprise when I found my fuzzy hand-raised lambs nibbling on dirt and rocks while the mothered lambs grazed serenely with the rest of the flock. I guessed they were probably trying to imitate the older sheep without the personal instruction and loving example a mother would provide. These deprived lambs watched a bunch of sheep heads down, eating, and did their best to copy what they saw. I have some pretty funny movies of my husband, his head down in the grass, pulling it up by the handful and feeding it to his favorite orphan, trying to get the point across (it finally worked!).

As Bethany said, "What do you expect when your mom's a bucket?"

She decided to teach those lambs to drink. Down on all fours, she crawled over to a bucket of water and demonstrated proper drinking technique. Bethany carefully lowered her pursed lips to the surface of the water and noisily slurped. The little ram lambs watched, then tried for themselves, bumping the bucket and causing some turbulence. They got water up their noses and ran away the first few times, but Bethany stayed with it, showing them over and over how it was done. And, yes, they finally figured it out and moved beyond their dependence on bottles and fear of the trough.

They needed an example. Someone to love them and show them how to live. They lacked a mother, but they had a shepherd.

I wonder if I look as foolish to God as my motherless lambs when I try to live my life by imitating the world around me. I see people working to accumulate possessions or gain approval. Money, popularity, comfort, convenience – these seem to be the goals of so many. Who or what affects the choices I make?

David knew who to follow.

He said:

O Lord, I give my life to you.
I trust in you, my God… show me the right path,
O Lord; point out the road for me to follow.
Lead me by your truth and teach me, for you are the God who saves me.
All day long I put my hope in you.
Remember, O Lord, your compassion and unfailing love, which you have shown from long ages past…
The Lord is good and does what is right;

He shows the proper path to those who go astray.
He leads the humble in doing right, teaching them his
way.
The Lord leads with unfailing love and faithfulness
all who keep his covenant and obey his demands.
For the honor of your name, O Lord, forgive my many,
many sins.
Who are these who fear the Lord?
He will show them the path they should choose.

PSALM 25:1, 4–6, 8–12, NLT

We can't learn how to live by watching the world around us. We need to learn to rely on our Shepherd to teach us his ways. If you read the Gospels, paying careful attention to the way Jesus lived and interacted with others, you have the perfect example to follow. See his kindness and patience. Notice his habit of withdrawing to be with the Father. Ask him to be your model. Allow the Holy Spirit to guide you and enable you to obey. Pay attention to those solid, committed Christians God places in your path and learn from them as well.

We are not alone.

Our progress in the Christian walk is not a do-it-yourself project.

Yes, we must be willing and teachable.

But God comes down to us, takes care of us.

(Thank God), we're not on our own.

I dare to believe that the luckless will get lucky someday in you.

You won't let them down: orphans won't be orphans forever.

Psalm 10:14b, The Message

Show me how you work, God: school me in your ways. Take me by the hand; lead me down the path of truth. You are my savior, aren't you?

Psalm 25:4–5, The Message

Heavenly Father,
Thank you for sending your Son.
He lived a human life before he died to save me.
He has made a way for me to follow
and he shows me the way.
Help me look to him.
Amen.

Now follow...

Play a little game this week. Imagine Jesus sitting alongside you in the car on your way to work. Or kneeling next to you as you pull weeds in the garden. You can talk to him if you like, but you don't have to. Just picture him there. After you have practiced this several times on your own, try imagining him next to you during your workday or at the grocery store.

Does playing this game affect your behavior?

Murray's Vanishing Mom

Murray was the only one of our lambs who was named by his mother. We go crazy every year naming the lambs, sometimes choosing a theme, like flowers or gemstones, for all the little ones. One memorable year, we used *The Cosby Show* and ended up with a barnyard full of memorable characters – Heathcliff, Claire, Theo, even Vanessa.

But Murray was named by his mother, moments after he was born, when she muttered her love language to her newborn, very clearly calling him "Mur-ur-ur-y… Murray." The name stuck.

Murray was a gorgeous jet-black ram lamb, but he had a blind spot.

Up.

Murray couldn't comprehend the concept.

At the time our sheep lived in a hundred-year-old hand-built barn designed for dairy cows. In order to get into the barn, the sheep jumped up two concrete steps and landed inside where they safely spent the night. Every evening at the same time, Bethany called the sheep in, promising, "Grain, girls!" and "Good hay, good hay!"

Murray's mom joined the group every night, with Murray tagging along behind. One by one every sheep jumped into the barn. But when Murray's mother made the leap, he didn't follow.

Instead, he panicked. He'd run frantically from side to side, looking for her and calling out to her. She'd come to the threshold and answer him, but Murray never looked up those twenty-four inches to see her there. We decided that in Murray's very tiny lamb brain, he perceived her jumping up into the barn as a disappearance. Mom was there one second and gone the next. He could hear her when he called, but she was now *invisible*.

Sometimes Murray's mom would leap back down out of the barn, scaring him all over again as she reappeared. She'd lead him back to the door, leap up, and thus, cruelly disappear again.

He never did get it.

One of us would eventually stop laughing long enough to catch the little guy and lift him into the barn where he was happily reunited with his mom.

Murray's perception of the world was his reality. It was also wrong. No relativism here, where what you believe is true for you, and you can have one truth while I can have another. Murray thought his mom could disappear and he was wrong – even though I'm pretty sure he didn't care a fig about ultimate truth.

119

He just wanted his mama.

In order to ensure just that, the shepherd caught him, then lifted him up to her.

It's a little like grace. Confused and frightened, lost and alone, we cry out, looking around us, trying to make sense of our circumstances. And, of course, we can't.

Praise God, grace doesn't depend on our understanding of it. We have a Shepherd who knows what we're like and loves us anyway. He is with us and has mercy on us. He comes all the way down to save us and bring us to himself.

Murray always seemed pretty grateful.

Our Lord is great, with limitless strength; we'll never comprehend what he knows and does.

PSALM 147:5, *THE MESSAGE*

I look to you, heaven-dwelling God, look up to you for
help.

PSALM 123:1, *THE MESSAGE*

Dear Lord,
Help me to admit my need for you.
Help me to come to you for help
or at least not to resist you.
Help me to follow you,
to stay close to you so I won't lose my way.
Lift me in your arms
and place me where you want me to be.
In Jesus' name, Amen.

120

Now follow...

Read Psalm 40 (in *The Message* version, if you have it). Do
what David did:
- Wait on God.
- Praise him.
- Give yourself over to him.
- Let his Word enter your life.
- Tell someone else about him.
- Trust him to help you.
- Realize that you're nothing and have nothing.
- Trust God to make something of you.

Bad at Math

Can a sheep sin?

Probably not in the classical sense.

But if you define sin as missing the mark – oh yeah.

Like us, they excel at that.

Today Gilda has done wrong. She made a wrong choice, caused harm, and ultimately condemned herself.

A mistaken perception, a faulty premise – then Gilda opposed her shepherd, getting her own way in the here and now, but losing everything in the end.

And I grieved.

Here's what happened: Gilda gave birth to two beautiful ewe lambs. In our flock twins are common and God equipped sheep to raise two lambs easily. Gilda gave birth without incident, then licked and spoke softly to both lambs soon afterwards. Gilda, like all mama sheep, recognized her own smell on the fluid-slick babies. Bonding initially appeared to be going well.

The next day I noticed Gilda stood patiently while her first lamb, Sparrow, nursed, but danced away when Magpie, the second, tried to do the same. I felt the little one's teeth. *Not too sharp*, I thought, but filed them smoother anyway to be sure they weren't cutting into the ewe.

I pushed Magpie in the right direction and she began to nurse, but as soon as her mother sniffed the baby, she kicked and pulled away. I held her still so Magpie could get a good long drink and then went to the house for my bag of tricks. I tried applying vanilla extract to Magpie's tail and Gilda's nose. No dice.

Sheep instinctively guard their milk supply for their own lambs and won't allow strange lambs to nurse. Sometimes they "can't count to two" and choose one of their babies to be their own and deem the other one "not theirs."

It happens.

Vicks VapoRub® didn't work either. I got out the stanchion. This is a wooden contraption that imprisons the ewe. She can lie down and stand up, but can't turn her head back to see which lamb is nursing. Gilda bucked and fought a little but finally settled down and both lambs ate. I trudged back to the house through the melting snow and laid down for a nap.

Two hours later, I found the stanchion on its side with Gilda still in it. I untangled her and checked for injuries. She wasn't hurt and hadn't crushed her lambs, so I held her still again so Magpie could eat. I should have tied her but since she wasn't harassing Magpie at the time, I left them, hoping for the best.

I could hear the thumping from the mud-room door at the next barn check. Gilda was pounding her cute little

spotted lamb into the barn wall. I rescued Magpie, proclaimed her a bottle lamb and put her in a pen of her own. She looked fine until the next day when my husband found her dead.

Internal injuries? I don't know. I was too tired and sad to do a post-mortem at that point. Gilda was a good mother to her remaining lamb, but was marked to be culled from the flock because I can't keep sheep who are bad at math.

So, no, Gilda didn't think what she was doing was wrong or evil. She wasn't consciously disobeying (as if a sheep could obey). Still, Gilda withheld her love. She held back and resisted all my efforts to show her what to do.

My way.

Not yours.

We say it to God, just like Gilda.

Our hearts rebel.

We close our ears, our minds, and our hearts.

It's a picture of sin.

God grieves.

How can I know all the sins lurking in my heart?
Cleanse me from these hidden faults.

PSALM 19:12, NLT

Dear God,
I don't know where to start.
Sometimes I just want to do what I want.
It doesn't seem like sin. I just want my own way.
Is that so wrong? Apparently it is.
Help me to want your way.
To remember to ask for your direction.
In Jesus' name, Amen.

Now follow...

124 David, although known for his more obvious sins, also struggled with the problem of hidden sin – under-the-surface attitudes that aren't pleasing to God.

Read Psalm 19 slowly and thoughtfully. Notice how David begins with the vastness of God's world. He sings of the sun moving from one end of the heavens to the other – nothing is hidden from its heat (verse 6, NASB).

Then he sings about God's Word and its work in our lives. God's Word makes us wise, restores us, and satisfies us.

David concludes by asking God to keep him from sinning and to make his thoughts and words acceptable to the Lord, his rock and redeemer.

Having read the Psalm and considered it, now make it your prayer.

God is sure to answer this one.

What Vera Knew

Vera is an experienced ewe. This lambing season, however, her maternal instincts went haywire.

At the 11:00 p.m. barn check, I found Vera, one of two new mothers with single lambs. I reached down to strip her teats – squeeze out the waxy plugs so the milk would flow freely – and discovered that Vera was dry. She hadn't given birth yet but had stolen one of Claudia's twins. We repossessed the lamb and penned it with its real mama. Vera bellowed, trying to get to the lamb. We let her out, hoping she'd have her own babies soon.

Well, later that night, we found Vera contentedly cleaning off two new little lambs. Relieved, we dried them off and, just to be sure, checked to see if she was the mother.

She was not.

We found a timid first-time mom in the corner of the barn. Vera must have pushed her aside and adopted her babies. We placed these lambs with their mother, against Vera's vigorous protest.

Of course, there were consequences. Now that the

delicate bonding process had been disturbed, each of the real mothers rejected one of her twins.

But Vera was so sure she was right. How could the shepherd be so cruel as to take her babies away, not once, but twice?

Sometimes I too am sure I know the right thing to do. It's obvious – so much so that I don't think I need to ask God for direction or guidance. Like Vera, my perspective is flawed; what I "know" could be wrong.

And I'm not alone. Our society's belief that we can figure things out ourselves lets us venerate human wisdom and reject the idea that God could be a source of wisdom. Autonomy is everything in this school of thought. Relativism – you have your truth, I have mine, both equally valid – prevails when independence is paramount. Absolute truth seems impossible – even unnecessary. We're pretty sure we can get along without it.

It's foolishness.

William P. Young, author of *The Shack*, said, "For any created being, autonomy is lunacy. Freedom involves trust and obedience *inside* a relationship of love" (emphasis his).[15] We might wish it were different but it's not.

We can't do this on our own.

We need a Shepherd.

People, like sheep, are convinced that we know the truth and can decide by ourselves on the right course of action.

On our own, we can't.

Know this: God is God, and God, God. He made us; we
didn't make him. We're his people, his well-tended sheep.

PSALM 100:3, *THE MESSAGE*

Don't put your life in the hands of experts who know
nothing of life, of *salvation* life. Mere humans don't have
what it takes; when they die, their projects die with them.
Instead, get help from the God of Jacob, put your hope in
God and know real blessing!

PSALM 146:3–5, *THE MESSAGE*

Dear Lord,
Help me to realize I don't know it all – can't know it all.
Help me not to be ashamed to own you
as my source of wisdom and guidance.
Remind me to ask you for directions
even when I think I already know what to do.
Help me to trust in you and not myself.
Amen.

Now follow...

The Christian walk is countercultural. At first, consciously,
disregard the issue of what other people think – this is
ultimately between you and God. Try to concentrate on asking
God for his wisdom and guidance.

Listen.

Pray for discernment.

As this becomes a more regular practice for you, ask God to help you be open about his guidance and impact on your life as he gives you the opportunity.

He'll guide you in this too.

The Shepherd's Care

By now, you may realize that a lot goes into caring for sheep. Phillip Keller, in his well-known book, *A Shepherd Looks at the 23rd Psalm*,[16] contrasts a good shepherd's care with that of a negligent one. He makes it clear that there is a difference between having sheep and keeping sheep.

When I attended shearing school, I got up close and personal with a neglected flock. Their owner volunteered them for the neophyte shearers to practice on – his sheep were sheared at no cost to him, but were subjected to a bunch of beginners wielding unfamiliar – and very sharp – objects.

That right there may be a commentary on how much he cared for the well-being of his flock.

At first the sheep didn't look so bad because all that wool hid the truth of their emaciation. We found their protruding bones soon enough – no matter how we tried, we lacked the skill to separate them from their fleeces without occasionally drawing blood. We also saw evidence of keds or sheep ticks digging in and feasting here and there on these unlucky and unloved woolies.

David's 23rd Psalm summarizes the experience of a well-cared-for flock. Such sheep lack nothing. They enjoy lush pasture and graze safely under the shepherd's watchful eye. They find quiet pools of water – crucial because sheep drink not by lapping like a dog but by placing their mouth on the surface and creating a vacuum to draw the water in – like sucking on a straw. Sheep could die of thirst right next to running water – they wouldn't be able to drink it. If they tried, the water would go up their noses since they're just barely above their mouths. If sheep don't have access to clean, still water, they'll drink muddy standing water, full of liver flukes and bacteria.

Sheep need clean water, still water – lots of water.

In order to get them to drink the right amount as well as to supply trace nutrients, we offer them mineral salt to make them thirsty. A balanced diet, including plenty of water, is crucial in keeping sheep healthy and productive.

Our sheep are fed by pasture rotation – a system of portable net fencing that parcels off a section of new fresh grass every few days. This helps keep the sheep free of parasites and leaves the land better for the use. They fertilize the soil, their small, round droppings falling between the blades of grass close to the ground, where they break down and enrich the soil. A "cool" manure, sheep dung is safe for even the most fragile plants. The sheep's hooves aerate the soil, leaving healthy grass and a park-like setting. Well-pastured sheep benefit the soil, but only if they're constantly moving ahead. Left too long in one place, they overgraze, destroying roots and causing erosion.

Besides their physical requirements, sheep need security. Delicious and defenseless, they need to be safe from predators. Wolves, cougars, bears, and, here in the Midwest, coyotes all enjoy making a meal of a wandering or unprotected sheep.

Less obvious than these are smaller creatures that torture and kill neglected sheep. Summer brings flies that harass the flock and internal parasites that sap their strength. One kind of fly, the nasal bot, invades the sheep's nasal passages and lays eggs up there, leaving them to hatch and take up residence inside their heads, nearly driving them mad. When the flies are at their worst, the sheep scatter and run, hiding their noses in each other's wool or a patch of grass for protection.

They can't graze in peace or digest their food, so they quickly lose condition without our help. Every few weeks we apply an oily insecticide to their heads to repel the flies. Shepherds in David's time used oil mixed with sulphur and spices, anointing their heads with oil.

Sometimes relationship turmoil causes unrest in the flock. Fighting between sheep can get the whole flock so stirred up that they are unable to rest and to ruminate. Often, just the shepherd's presence and observation can cause tensions to subside. The sheep stop focusing on each other when the shepherd is nearby and look to him instead. If some sheep fail to do this, the shepherd may closely confine them and cover their eyes with hoods so they can't butt each other; or when all efforts fail, he may make the painful decision to remove a troublemaker from the flock.

Sheep, like most animals who live in groups, have a "pecking order." Stronger, more willful sheep hog the feeders, pushing smaller, weaker animals away. Here again, the shepherd needs to intervene, coming up with creative feeding techniques that prevent the harm caused by friction in the flock.

Peace – heartsease – is necessary for health and growth.

What happens when sheep are cared for poorly? They fail to thrive and end up scrawny and sick. Even mild mismanagement shows up in their wool, our farm's income source. Any stress on the sheep – they may have been ill, chased by dogs, or couldn't keep up with the demands of a triplet pregnancy – can cause a weak spot in the fleece. When threatened, the sheep sends its nutritional resources to the place of greatest need – fighting illness, growing lambs, or running in fear – whatever. She may survive looking pretty good but the fleece, ruined by the break, tells the rest of the story.

Actions, or their absence, have consequences.

The quality of the shepherd's care is apparent in his sheep. Their condition says as much about the shepherd as themselves.

The shepherd provides the care.

The sheep submits to it.

That's all.

Accepts it.

Some sheep find this hard.

Some people do too.

Though the Lord is great, he cares for the humble...

PSALM 138:6A, NLT

He poured great draughts of water down parched throats:
the starved and hungry got plenty to eat.

PSALM 107:9, *THE MESSAGE*

133

O Good Shepherd,
I don't really recognize everything you do to care for me.
Thank you for caring for me anyway.
Show me when I am being a troublesome sheep,
and let your presence be enough to make me stop.
Please make yourself evident in my life –
let people see the Shepherd when they look at me.
In Jesus' name I ask this, Amen.

Now follow...

Ask God to show you the methods you use to resist or avoid him.

Listen for his answers.

Consider the truth of them.

Offer them back to him.

Lay them down.

Look for opportunities to give in to his care. The answers will be different for everyone and may be as simple as taking a nap or opening your Bible.

Give in.

Be his sheep.

Flocking

After the lambs have been weaned and the ewes have bulked up again, we separate the breeding ewes from the yearlings we keep for breeding stock. These young maidens require little in the way of care and keep their own society. Less tame than the group we interact with daily, they move in formation like birds wheeling through the sky. We refer to them as "the school of fish" and enjoy the daily ballet they perform on their grassy emerald stage.

Sheep stay together (or flock) by nature. This built-in flocking instinct can be so strong that sheep coming down with something will struggle to stay with the group until they're sick enough to be past help. We won't sell single sheep to a spinner or beginning shepherd, no matter how insistent. "Lone sheep" don't act right. Seeing no one like themselves, they often copy the family dog or cat. Sometimes they mope or refuse to eat.

Sheep just need other sheep. Some of them enjoy hanging out with certain other sheep, forming smaller groups of friends within the larger ovine culture. Each one is safer as part of the larger group. Oily glands above their hooves scent the grass as they pass, making it easier for them to stay together, but this doesn't explain their mysterious dance.

If one sheep is off by itself, you can be sure something's wrong.

Like those in labor, sick sheep eventually separate themselves from the flock.

People do this too.

The very abnormal among us can't relate to others at all. The serial killer's neighbors all say the same thing: "He was a quiet man... kept to himself."

On a more ordinary scale, physical illness, depression, hurt feelings, anxiety – these can cause us to withdraw from others.

136

It's the wrong move.

Sheep, like people, are relational beings. Despite the differences in our personalities, all of us, introvert or extrovert, need other people. God doesn't call us to a religion of isolation. Learning to get along, caring for each other – relating – is the training ground for our God-walk. Gathering with others at church puts us in proximity with others who can be models for growth, support in times of trouble, leaders when we need direction, even irritants who provide us with opportunities to practice forgiveness. David said, "I will give thee thanks in the great congregation: I will praise thee among much people" (Psalm 35:18, KJV).

A sheep alone is stressed or sick, and extremely vulnerable. These are the ones predators target, capitalizing on their weaknesses.

Sometimes I'm tempted to withdraw from others when I'm sad, disappointed or exhausted. If I pull myself away from others when I'm weak, I leave myself open to the enemy of my soul. Like my sheep, I may need to make the effort to stay with my friends who can surround me with love and their prayers.

When I am undone – unable to stay with the flock – I can be reassured that my Shepherd is watching. He loves me and sees my distress. He comes to me and lifts me up, bringing me back to the fold.

137

> God places the lonely in families; he sets the prisoners free and gives them joy.
>
> PSALM 68:6, NLT

> How wonderful it is, how pleasant, when brothers live together in harmony!
>
> PSALM 133:1, NLT

Heavenly Father,
help me to see beyond myself.
Keep me from doing the easy or comfortable thing —
pulling away, nursing that grudge,
protecting that old wound.
Help me instead to walk in fellowship with your people,
loving them as they are, like you do.
In Jesus' name, Amen.

Now follow...

138 The Christian life would be easier to live if it weren't for the people.

Makes it tempting to go it alone.

Don't be fooled. Ask God to remind you that this kind of thinking is a trap and a deception. Pulling away from others may provide instant relief, but it makes us even weaker and more vulnerable. Ask God to help you to stay "out there" even when it's hard.

Be on alert for others who have withdrawn from fellowship. Pray about visiting them, sending a card, letting them know that you care and want to help.

Then do it.

Ram Vigilance

Soon after each tiny lamb slides into the world, as soon as I'm sure it's breathing, I check for gender. I want to know early on which of the little ones are ram lambs. Farms, you see, are not gender-neutral, equal-opportunity establishments. Ewe lambs are likely to stay in my flock longer for breeding and wool production. A farm our size needs just one ram for procreation. We may keep a pair of ram lambs to show and sell them as breeding stock if they do well. The other males are wethered, destined to be food for the family, or for the church's Seder supper, or for friends who buy locker lambs for meat. Occasionally we have such an abundance of ram lambs that we take a trailer-load to market where they're sold.

Their eventual destination is not the reason for my curiosity so soon after birth. I need to know which are male so that I can handle them in ways that make them less dangerous as adults.

The nature channels on TV show wild rams backing up, then running full tilt at each other, lowering their chins and cracking their horned heads together. All of us have seen cartoons with rams charging at and butting Daffy Duck or Bugs Bunny. A charging ram in real life, though, is no laughing matter.

One of the first bits of sheep advice we got starting out was "Never turn your back on a ram."

We listened. Our first ram, J.J., reinforced it by running at us as soon as he heard the gate open. It was tempting to turn tail and run, but unwise. Rams run faster than people, so unless we were close to an exit, the tail we turned presented a perfect target for J.J. We went out to the paddock armed with garbage-can lids (a satisfying *thwock*); a squirt gun (pepper spray might have worked better); and, like Teddy Roosevelt, we ended up walking softly and carrying a big stick.

J.J. didn't stay very long. Our daughter was only in fifth grade, and at over 200 pounds J.J. was too formidable an adversary for her at chore time. He fathered our first lambs and then we followed the advice of more experienced shepherds in handling our ram lambs. We did not pet them on the head. When we had to touch them, we held them under the jaw. We didn't allow anyone to taunt or tease the rams. We never tried to be friends with them. We'd been told that rams shouldn't be socialized, but should remain a little afraid of people, running away when approached rather than running to greet. We were told, and still believe, that the most dangerous rams are bottle-fed orphans who, of course, are very familiar with people. On our farm, bottle-fed males are wethered or go to market before they can become a problem.

Young rams are best left alone.

The lessons we learned about ram vigilance were

reinforced periodically. An older shepherd a few miles from our place turned his back on his Suffolk ram for just a moment during chores. The ram crushed both of his thigh-bones, putting him in the hospital, then into months of rehab. He considered himself lucky.

A few years back, the shepherd community was rocked by the news of the deaths of two elderly shepherds in China Grove, North Carolina. No one will ever know for sure what happened after Carl and Mary Katherine Beaver drove up to feed their sheep one afternoon in the fall of 2000. Neighbors and their nephew became concerned when the car was still parked there two hours later. They found Mary Katherine dead and Carl near death. The couple had bought a new ram a few weeks before and had recently moved him into the group. When rescuers arrived, all of the sheep retreated from the men except the new ram, who approached. The 250-pound ram had blood on its head and back. The couple's nephew, who owned a nearby ranch, said rams "can get especially aggressive if they become too tame and have no fear of people."

Carl Beaver died the next morning.[17]

Something I heard Joni Earickson Tada say once in a talk stuck in my mind and shakes loose whenever I care for the new ram babies on our farm. She said, "Don't domesticate your sins."[18]

Don't domesticate your sins.

The ram lambs are cute and appealing at first. They're harmless at that point – wobbly-legged, ten-or-so pounds, wagging their little tails. What's the harm in cuddling them? I have to remind myself that little lambs become big rams and keep my hands in my pockets when I'm tempted to scratch their heads.

God help me to be just as cautious with each "what's the harm?" temptation I encounter outside the barn.

Don't let me drift toward evil or take part in acts of wickedness. Don't let me share in the delicacies of those who do wrong.

PSALM 141:4, NLT

The wicked have set a snare for me, but I have not strayed from your precepts.

PSALM 119:110, NIV

143

Heavenly Father,
make me wise to the dangers of temptation.
Show me that I lack the wisdom to foresee
the eventual outcome of what seems attractive to me.
Warn me, Lord.
Then make me strong to heed your warning.
Keep me from snares.
In Jesus' name, Amen.

Now follow...

This week, spend some time examining the activities you choose to do. Do some of them bring you closer to the Lord?

Draw you farther away? Do you make excuses to yourself for some of the things you do? Or some of the games you play or websites you visit? What about the books you read or movies you watch – do any of these feed appetites that may not please God? (I'm not suggesting a guilt-fest – just asking.)

Prayerfully consider.

Now seek to please God in every part of your life.

Naked in Winter

While most shepherds shear in the spring, we have our sheep sheared in the dead of winter. Seems kind of mean, doesn't it – taking off their wooly warmth just when they need it most? Oh, and it does get cold here on the prairie. Twenty-six below. And that's without the wind-chill from the Alberta Clippers that sweep down unimpeded across the open plains. Why would we want to leave our sheep unprotected in weather like that?

To save their lambs – that's why.

You have to understand that our well-wooled sheep are pretty comfortable in even the coldest weather. Wool insulates beautifully and our sheep's heavy fleeces place six to nine inches of it between their skin and the stormy blasts. That's a pretty thick winter coat! The ability to ignore the cold is great for the ewes but not so great for their soaking-wet newborns who, because their mamas are comfortable outside, end up being born in a snowdrift and freezing to death.

Removing their warm fleeces allows the sheep to feel the cold and, because they know the truth about the temperature, they seek shelter. Instead of making decisions based on bad information ("It's not so cold out here"), the naked sheep naturally move out of the wind and killing cold. They go into the barn when the mercury falls, and the lambs have a better chance of surviving.

Now, I know we don't actually make our sheep any smarter by shearing them. But they act more wisely when they know what is true. They do, as my mother used to say, have enough sense to come in out of the cold. And a shepherd can use that to get the right response.

Is there a lesson here? (Isn't there always?)

My sheep don't like being shorn, no matter when it's done. It involves a lot of things they don't enjoy – missing breakfast; being confined, then restrained; hearing the scary noise of the shearing machine; occasionally getting nicked; and finally not recognizing all their old pals (at least at first). Add to that our flock's shock at being involved in an involuntary ovine version of the "Polar Plunge" – trust me, shearing day doesn't rank nearly as high on the sheep's hit parade as the first day on pasture or fall's annual reintroduction of grain. They don't like it. They don't understand it. And they can't prevent it.

What good could come of this?

Only truth.

Wisdom.

Life.

Hope for the future.

The Psalms tell us, "The Lord knows the thoughts of man, that they are but a breath" (Psalm 94:11, ESV). David,

the shepherd-king, knew that although God understands our thoughts, we can never hope to fully understand his. "Your thoughts – how rare, how beautiful! God, I'll never comprehend them" (Psalm 139:17, *The Message*).

Now, I can't really know what my sheep are thinking when they lose their winter coats. I'm pretty sure, however, that they don't know what I'm thinking. The good news is that they don't need to. I am caring for them in a way that makes them *act* wise.

We can trust that God is doing the same for us.

Surely you desire truth in the inner parts; you teach me wisdom in the inmost place.

PSALM 51:6, NIV

Take me by the hand; lead me down the path of truth. You're my Savior, aren't you?

PSALM 25:5, *THE MESSAGE*

Dear God,
Sometimes everything seems to be too much.
I give up. I surrender.
I don't know why it's so hard for me to believe
that you can arrange the circumstances of my life
so that I can do what is right.
When you can, make me wise.
And when I am not wise,
you have my permission to do whatever it takes
to accomplish your will in my life.
In Jesus' name I pray, Amen.

Now follow...

Pray God to show you if there is anything in the way of your knowing his will (or doing it). Listen for his answer. Ask God for wisdom – then pay attention to the thoughts that run through your mind. Don't be surprised if you feel confused. You may want to talk about this prayer with a respected Christian friend.

And if God shows you an impediment, surrender it to him.

Remembering Wren

Yesterday Wren died. We lose the sheep we love the most – or maybe it only seems that way. Wren was, of course, my favorite ewe, loved from the day she was born. And her ewe lamb, one of twins, was the only lamb we lost this year, tangled and strangled in a fence. Wren was only two and had shown great promise, twinning her first time and mothering the lambs as well as any of my more experienced ewes. When her lamb died, I was sad but consoled myself with the thought of all her future lambing seasons, her beautiful genetics improving the flock.

No more.

We found Wren leaning against the barn on a hot summer evening, weak and barely able to stand. Her temperature was 107° so we cooled her by hosing down her legs and the skin of her "armpits." Mike and I helped her into the barn, offered her a drink and some hay, and gave her an antibiotic.

She seemed a little better.

The way she looked in the morning dashed all hope. She was lying down balanced on her chest, her head still up;

but she stared straight ahead without blinking, unaware that a fly had touched down lightly on the moist surface of her right eye. Wren's mouth gaped, saliva trailing into a pool on the straw.

Hope gone, I went into damage-control mode, wanting to save the rest of the flock. I called the vet for his take on this previously healthy sheep's sudden decline. After hearing my assessment, he asked to see stool samples from Wren and the unaffected sheep in the flock right away, so I collected specimens and set out for Canton twenty miles away. The samples were negative.

Wren died while I was gone.

Doc Hahn wanted an autopsy but Mike had the pickup at work and my Buick couldn't transport a 200-pound ewe. With the temperature in the nineties we couldn't wait another day.

Mike buried her when he got home.

I walked the pasture comparing pictures of toxic plants to the dry, dusty vegetation underfoot. Sheep laurel, rhododendron, lupine – I came up empty and decided to reopen the grazing land to the rest of the flock.

We'll never know for sure why she died. Doc Hahn's best guess was heat stroke.

I waited until I was alone to cry. I don't feel much like a farmer when I cry over the death of my animals. My stoic Midwestern neighbors would laugh if they knew, but I'm more shepherd than farmer. I love my sheep. Still, they aren't pets – more like co-workers – living in a relationship that results in the beautiful multihued wool for which our flock is known.

If it were in my power I would have saved her. But I couldn't.

We believe in God, all-powerful, all-wise, all-knowing, everywhere present. This presents a problem because, as we all know, sometimes God lets the bad thing happen.

This question – why a loving God allows bad things to happen – keeps a fair number of people from coming to God and maybe a larger number from fully trusting him. My little sheep tragedies pale beside the stories so many of us could tell.

"If God loves me and he could have stopped that drunk driver from taking the life of my child, but he chose not to – who needs him anyway?"

"And if everything happens for a reason – well then, tell me what it is!"

Books have been written and sermons preached to try to explain the intricacies of free will and God's plan for mankind. I've read some of them and might come close to understanding a few.

I heard a pastor on the radio say that we are all like

ants crawling across a Rembrandt painting. Seeing brown, we think the entire world is brown, until the ground under our tiny legs changes to green and later red or blue. Like the ant, we see the change in our circumstances, but we can't begin to grasp the concept of the artist's work (or even the existence of the painting itself). We're too small and close to the detail (and ants do have very tiny brains). The whole thing is beyond us.

I don't know why I find this so comforting.

Maybe because it sets me free from the obligation to explain God to myself (much less anyone else).

Here's what I *do* know:

God is loving. As high as heaven is over the earth, so strong is his love to those who fear him (Psalm 103:11, *The Message*).

And he is strong. David knew it and called to God, his Lord and strong Savior, for help.[19]

Maybe, like David, I'll be rescued from my enemies. God is able to do that and he longs for me to turn to him in my troubles. If he does come to my rescue, I'll thank him and rejoice.

And if he doesn't?

I'll thank him and rejoice.

He knows what is best.

And he doesn't have to make sense to me.

Wren is gone. She left no heritage. When I finish telling you about her I'll look for her fleece and pull it from the ones going out to be mill-spun. I think I'll wash it myself. Mike may want to comb her wool before I spin it, both of us passing our hands through the softness of the only thing she left behind.

I don't know what the yarn will become.
I will pray for God to show me.

The Lord cares deeply when his loved ones die.

PSALM 116:15, NLT

Be brave. Be strong. Don't give up. Expect God to get here soon.

PSALM 31:24, *THE MESSAGE*

Dear Heavenly Father,
thank you for your unchanging love.
Help me to trust you and thank you
for all that you bring into my life.
Make me strong because I trust in you.
I don't see the big picture
but I'm sure you have everything under control.
In Jesus' name, Amen.

154

Now follow...

Remember a time when you were disappointed in God. Or prayed for something and got something else. Talk to God about your disappointment. Think about loving God not for what he has to offer you but because of who he is. He loves us that purely. Ask him to help you to love him for himself.

Bunny Faces the Enemy

Bunny (I don't remember how she came by that name) was a brave sheep.

An ebony sheep with long curly wool, Bunny had what livestock judges call good conformation. She had straight, well-muscled legs; a long, level rump; a substantial loin; and great bone structure. As sheep go, Bunny was a knockout. Although she inspired admiration, she (being a sheep) didn't inspire fear.

We discovered her courage when she first lambed. She had given birth to twins, one black and one white. At the time, we had our first Great Pyrenees guard dog. Goliath had been raised from a pup alongside the sheep and, like all guardian-breed dogs, considered himself one of the flock. In addition to patrolling the fence line all night long to keep the coyotes at bay, he checked the scent of each new member of the flock soon after birth, taking roll and assuming responsibility for each new addition. When Goliath came to welcome Bunny's babies into the flock, her eyes widened. She saw him not as a protector, but as a dog – the enemy.

She stomped her front foot at him. He calmly looked back at her, tipping his head to one side, wondering why she didn't recognize him as an old friend. She lowered her head to charge, but confined in a five-foot-by-five-foot lambing pen, she couldn't gain the needed momentum. She stomped her foot again; then tried to jump the panel. With her attention focused on the dog, she didn't notice me moving to stand behind her. I waved my hand to catch Goliath's eye, then shooed him away as Bunny held the ground between her babies and the enemy. Goliath retreated and Bunny fairly strutted as she turned back to her lambs.

I left the barn that day thinking about how I stand to face my enemy. Bunny may not have known how outclassed she was that day. Dogs kill sheep – never the reverse. Yet she didn't quail when she thought she and her family were threatened. She stood and faced the enemy with all she had. Had the dog wanted to hurt her, it would have been no contest. Still, she allowed her heart to be courageous. Her shepherd stood behind her, fighting the battle and bringing her victory.

She reminded me of a shepherd boy who faced another, more famous Goliath who certainly intended to do him harm. David saw his enemy, but he *knew* his God. He faced the giant without armor, knowing God was with him, giving him victory. He trusted the Lord to deliver the enemy into his hands. The battle didn't depend on the weapons at hand – "for not in my bow do I trust, nor can my sword save me" (Psalm 44:6, ESV). The battle belonged to the Lord – as it always does, even to this day.

I often forget this and go through life imagining that each

battle is my own. Western culture's emphasis on achievement has seeped into my psyche, making me think my successes belong to me and are earned by my own efforts. Thinking like this might work for a while, but in the end I find myself tired and afraid. I can't do it all, be everything to everyone, but still I spend myself in the attempt. Like Bunny, I imagine that my tiny efforts won the day, rather than acknowledging that God is at work in my life.

What then? Do I do nothing, expecting God to step up and save the day?

No. Of course not.

The rest of the Israelites stood by when Goliath taunted them and their God. They cowered in fear while young David stepped out in faith, realizing that he had a part to play, knowing his God would stand behind him.

I don't know why God, being all-powerful, chooses to act through broken and imperfect people. You can see it all

through the Bible. God works in us and through us to get his will done. We, too, are part of his plan and he wants us to offer ourselves to him – to "delight to do his will" (Psalm 40:8, NASB).

If we think the mission is too big for us, we're right.

It is.

And God knows it is.

But we are here and we are his.

We can step up and do what seems so hard to us. We can be brave and let our hearts take courage because of who God is. God will not let us down.

Be strong, and *let* your heart take courage.

PSALM 27:14, ESV (EMPHASIS MINE)

The king is not saved by his great army; a warrior is not delivered by his great strength. The war horse is a false hope for salvation, and by its might cannot rescue. Behold, the eye of the Lord is on those who fear him, on those who hope in his steadfast love, that he may deliver their soul from death and keep them alive in famine.

PSALM 33:16–19, ESV

Dear Lord,
help me both to be bold in your strength
and to realize that it is your strength that sustains me.
You are so gracious and understanding when I fail.
Make my actions pleasing to you and use me in your service.
In Jesus' name I pray, Amen.

Now follow...

This week, read Psalm 91, the Warrior's Psalm, every morning. Notice the promises God makes in this Psalm. He is our shelter, our refuge and fortress. God delivers us, covers us. His faithfulness shields us. We don't need to be afraid because he protects us. Because we love him and know his name, God promises to be with us – to rescue, honor and satisfy us. Let these promises thrill you.

And let your heart take courage.

Lamb Races

Every year it happens – with every crop of lambs. They don't learn this behavior, but it happens without fail.

The lambs, ordinarily bouncy and nimble, hold still in synchrony, like racers waiting for the crack of the starter's pistol. Then, as if they'd heard it split the silence, they take off as one, running a route they somehow magically know. West toward the setting sun they scamper, around an abandoned rubber bucket – a sharp right at the milk house – then skidding to a halt at their finish line, their placidly grazing mamas.

The wonder of it!

Joy. Pure joy.

And I am privileged to see it.

These wooly creatures, mere weeks old, leap and gambol with every molecule inside them. Watching them gives me goosebumps.

I'm not the only one who feels it. Sometimes when one of them bounces past an old ewe, she forgets herself for a moment and joins in, launching her bulk upwards once or maybe twice, before she remembers her age and station in life and quickly returns to her grazing.

How do the lambs know a race is about to begin?

And their simultaneous but silent start – how do they manage that?

Are they really joyful, celebrating the beauty of their world?

Or am I just attributing human feelings to animals incapable of feeling them?

Scientists argue over whether animals experience emotions, but to me the lambs' play looks gleeful. The grass is new, green, and abundant. The air is crisp and full of exciting odors. The sun shines down, warming their curly coats. Their mothers are nearby, occupied but attentive to the sound of each lamb's voice.

They are safe.

The world is wonderful beyond words.

The lambs *need* to leap and frisk about. To celebrate. To worship.

So do we.

Maybe the world around us is darker than the one my lambs find themselves in. Some of us struggle with the tragic and unimaginable things we encounter in our work. Others encounter difficulties that make celebration unlikely. Almost all of us watch the news and wonder at our world.

Despite what discourages us, hope can be found if we look for it.

And with it, joy.

Notice the beauty of God's world – the tiny flower in the sidewalk crevice or majestic mountain peaks. Start to observe

162

the small beauties right in the middle of our ordinary lives: the smiles we give each other; kindness shown and small comforts given. If you don't find beauty by looking around you, look up. "God is sheer beauty, all-generous in love, loyal always and ever" (Psalm 100:5, *The Message*).

When my lambs race, they let what's inside them out. They obey the psalmist's command to "shout for joy to the Lord, *all the earth*" (Psalm 100:1, NIV, emphasis mine). I enjoy it and I imagine God enjoys it too.

We, too, can learn to praise him, expressing ourselves in any number of ways. Psalm 73 suggests music, both instrumental and vocal, and for those less musical, well, there's shouting. I'm blessed to live far enough from my neighbors that my shouts of joy don't disturb them.

However you do it, praise God from the heart, and with your whole heart. Psalm 45 begins, "My heart bursts its banks, spilling beauty and goodness. I pour it out in a poem to the King, shaping the river into words" (verse 1, *The Message*).

Put yourself into it. Forget what you look like or sound like. Turn off your inner critic. Praise is for God. Think about my little lambs, running as fast as their legs will carry them, springing high at random places on their racetrack, raising a dust as they round the corners, every now and then energizing another, infecting them with the intensity of their joy.

Praise like that.

Let me run loose and free, celebrating God's great work, every bone in my body laughing, singing, "God, there's no one like you."

PSALM 35:9, *THE MESSAGE*

163

He taught me how to sing the latest God-song, a praise-song to our God. More and more people are seeing this: they enter the mystery, abandoning themselves to God.

PSALM 40:3, *THE MESSAGE*

Lord, here we are.
Life has taught us to be careful, to be in control.
Help us to lean into you, to forget ourselves in praise.
Teach us to see you and your beauty in this imperfect world.
Teach us to express our awe and delight in worship.
Teach us, please, to celebrate.
In Jesus' name, Amen.

Now follow...

What you do now depends a lot on your own personality and your previous experiences of worship. To start, try reading a praise Psalm out loud and with expression to God. Psalms 145, 147, 148, and 150 are almost entirely praise and would be a good place to start. Then, try something different – write a poem, sing along with the radio in your car, sculpt, dance, paint, or draw.

No one else has to see.

Worship, praise, and celebrate.

Throw yourself into it.

Paths — or Ruts?

Three barns stand in the paddock behind our house. Deep ruts split the snow between them, bearing silent witness to the daily migration of the sheep. When the snow melts and the soil changes to gumbo mud, my sheep walk the same trail even though better footing lies only two feet to either side. In the summer, grass grows everywhere but on these sheep-trails. Dust rises from their hooves as the sheep walk single-file to the north barn or back to the south. Over and over they choose the familiar route.

Maybe they do it because it worked before. They went this way yesterday and the day before and nothing bad happened. Maybe they're following the leader. Sheep, being uniquely gifted to follow, seem compelled to do so. Regardless of the reason, my sheep move in formation, nose to tail, across the barnyard, forming ruts by choosing over and over the well-known, the safe, the old ways.

The church I attend struggles with this. Maybe all churches, all Christians, do. We have a history filled with rich traditions. Our parents and their parents before them

have worshipped in this place and in this way. Our methods have worked before – surely they will work again. We want to do what is safe. And we hate disapproval. When we look for guidance we check to see what everyone else is doing. Then we measure the reactions of others to our choices. This tendency is nothing to be ashamed of. We do this from the moment we're born. We look around us to learn how to act. This is what we are – how we are made. But what we are isn't what we're called to be.

Jesus came to a religious world that was firmly established. Laws, big and small, covered almost every situation a person could find himself in. People knew, for the most part, what they were supposed to do. Their lives may not have been perfect, but the chosen people felt safe and comfortable in their walk with God. Their rituals, which were beautifully designed to foreshadow the coming Messiah, had become an end unto themselves. People assumed that because God had wanted them to follow these ways in the past, he would always require these things, in these ways. They were sure they knew the mind of God and understood what he wanted and how he would act.

Jesus came and shook things up.

He put the law in perspective – he was not about performance. Jesus was unpredictable, scary, a threat. He came not to make people comfortable with how they already lived, nor to reinforce a set of rules which, if kept, contractually obligated God to fulfill his promises. Knowing that humans could never truly keep these rules or carry these burdens, Jesus called his people instead to follow him. To follow him instead of trusting the paths they'd been walking so long. To step away from the familiar, the safe, the outward form of the law and exchange it for the inward response to God (call it faith) that has always been the basis for a relationship with the God of the Universe.

Jesus didn't come to throw out the law. Indeed, he came to fulfill it. He demonstrated the heart of God to us.

He loves us.

And he calls us.

"Follow me," he says, calling us to move our eyes from the sheep in front of us, from the path we have always walked, to himself.

He calls us to himself.

We are to answer, to keep company with him, to notice where he is going and to move with him in that direction.

The path is no longer the rut in the ground in front of us;

it is the direction he is moving. He is the Shepherd who leads;
we fix our eyes on him and stay at his side.

The shepherd is calling.

Step out of that rut.

I'll run the course you lay out for me if you'll just show
me how. God, teach me lessons for living so I can stay the
course. Give me insight so I can do what you tell me – my
whole life one long, obedient response.

PSALM 119:32–34, THE MESSAGE

What a God! His road stretches straight and smooth.
Every God-direction is road-tested. Everyone who runs
toward him makes it.

PSALM 18:30, THE MESSAGE

168

Dear God,
I don't mean to go my own way.
Most of the time I'm secure in my belief
that my Christian habits are sufficient.
I confess that I forget to look to you for guidance.
I remain unaware of my need for you.
I'm not listening for your voice or seeking your face.
Don't give up on me.
Help me to step out of what's comfortable
and into your will.
In Jesus' name I pray, Amen.

Now follow...

This week, consider your faith walk. Which actions are habits? Which are disciplines? Which are responses to guidance as revealed in scripture or a "nudge" in your spirit? Which are done because of other people's opinions?

What is your motivation?

Do you believe God wants to guide you?

Do you believe he can?

Reread Psalm 119:32–34. Consider committing it to memory.

Like Sheep

I've spent many years as a Christian, studying my Bible and trying to live in the light of the Word. I pretty much fail spectacularly at it. Trying harder just doesn't make me any better at the Christian walk.

Since human effort doesn't cut it, there has to be some other way to live that works – that pleases God. Bill Griffiths, co-author of a beautiful book on forgiveness,[20] tells a story about a sheep that he bought as a pet in an attempt to learn more about God and his relationship with people. The fact that he lived in Long Island didn't deter him. Bill named the sheep Matthew and walked with him every day. This sheep went all around the neighborhood with him, staying close on his heels, focused on his owner (I don't know if Mr. Griffiths considered himself as a shepherd).

One day a police officer spotted them out for a stroll and insisted that Bill put the sheep on a leash. Although he knew it was unnecessary, Bill complied. But when he tried to walk Matthew on a leash, everything changed. Matthew no longer followed hard on Bill's heels. Instead, the 200-pound pet sheep walked at the length of the leash – twelve feet away. When Bill took the leash off, Matthew again followed him. Right behind him. With the leash back on, Matthew walked as far away as the leash allowed.

Puzzled by the behavior of his sheep, Bill asked God for insight. He already knew that sheep follow naturally. When Matthew was constrained and distracted by the leash, he lost his focus on the shepherd. This shift in focus rendered him unable to follow.

The leash gave Matthew too much to think about. Instead of watching Bill and sticking closely to him, the sheep was forced to consider the leash. This was very hard for the sheep and distanced him from the shepherd. Instead of staying close to his shepherd just because he loved him, Matthew was staying close because of an external force.

The leash turned joy into an effort.

Trying to "get it right" has never worked for anyone but Jesus, who had the advantage of being God himself. Jesus fulfilled the law for us and calls us now to walk with him.

Trying to live the Christian life as if it is a set of rules to follow or a daily to-do list is an exercise in frustration.

Well meant, like Matthew's leash, but doomed to fail.

I've been following Jesus for more than thirty years.

I'm not always sure where he is leading me.

Sometimes I even doubt that he *is* leading me.

When I look back on those years, though, I can see where he's led me. Every so often he reassures me that I'm right where he wants me, doing just what he wants. I'm never 100 per cent sure of his guidance ahead of time, but I'm 100 per cent sure of my Shepherd.

He is leading me just like he promised.

I know he's my Shepherd.

I know I'm his sheep.

That relationship, and not anything I attempt or achieve, is the key to this walk. Many Christians have discovered this secret. Oswald Chambers said, "The main thing about Christianity is not the work we do, but the relationship we maintain and the atmosphere produced by that relationship. That is all God asks us to look after and it is the one thing that is continually being assailed."[21]

And it is assailed. We are pulled in so many directions by our desires or fears, our busy schedules or our secret sins. Even though we long for God, we find ourselves wandering off after this or that.

We find out that we're incapable even of maintaining the connection.

But wait – still more good news! God does even that for us – "Day after day he carries us along" (Psalm 68:19, *The Message*).

Hear this poem by Joseph Bayly:

A Psalm of Wandering

Lord You know
I'm such a stupid sheep.
I worry
about all sorts of things
whether I'll find grazing land
still cool water
a fold at night in which I can feel safe.
I don't.
I only find troubles
want
loss.

I turn aside from you

173

to plan my rebel way.
I go astray.
I follow other shepherds
even other stupid sheep.
Then when I end up
on some dark mountain
cliffs before
wild animals behind
I start to bleat
Shepherd Shepherd
find me save me
or I die
And you do.[1]

174

The Shepherd saves us. Our lives and their living are in his hands and he will never let us down.[22] God's Spirit lives and breathes in us so we can walk with him, abide in him – follow him all the days of our lives.

Eyes on Jesus, following hard after him – this is the Christian walk. Watching the Shepherd, doing what I see him doing – it's so simple that I feel like there must be more to it. But whenever I add to it, I ruin it and can't walk the walk.

Simple – maybe.

Easy?

Not.

But it can be done.

"Walking with God" is a powerful figure of speech used to describe people in tune with him. Sheep, gifted at following,

1. ©1995, 2005 Cook Communications Ministries. **Psalms of My Life** by Joseph Bayly. Used with permission. May not be further reproduced.

express intimacy by walking with their shepherd.

We, the sheep of his hand, can do this too.

May our walk bring him great joy.

You're blessed when you stay on course, walking steadily on the road revealed by God. You're blessed when you follow his directions, doing your best to find him.

That's right – you don't go off on your own; you walk straight along the road he set.

You, God, prescribed the right way to live; now you expect us to live it.

PSALM 119:1–4, *THE MESSAGE*

I'm asking God for one thing, only one thing: to live with him in his house my whole life long. I'll contemplate his beauty; I'll study at his feet. That's the only quiet, secure place in a noisy world… When my heart whispered, "Seek God," my whole being replied, "I'm seeking him!"… Stay with God! Take heart. Don't quit. I'll say it again: Stay with God.

PSALM 27:4–5A, 8, 14, *THE MESSAGE*

Selah.

Now follow!

REFERENCES

1. Psalm 78:70–72.
2. Luke 9:23.
3. Psalm 81:13, NLT.
4. "Crafty Sheep Conquer Cattle Grids," BBC News, July 30, 2004. http://www.news.bbc.co.uk/1/hi/uk/3938591.stm. Accessed November 3, 2006.
5. Cobb, R., "An Introduction to Sheep Behavior," "Illini Sheep Net," January 22, 1999. http://www.traill.uiuc.edu/sheepnet/paperDisplay?ContentID=1. Accessed November 3, 2006.
6. Lewis, C. S., *The Four Loves*, New York: Harcourt, Brace, 1960, p. 121.
7. Psalms 74:2; 83:3; 94:5, The Message.
8. 1 Samuel 21:10–15.
9. Kendrick, K. M., daCosta, A. P., Leigh, A. E., Hinton, M. R., & Pierce, J. W., "Sheep Don't Forget a Face," *Nature* (404), November 8, 2001, pp. 165–6.
10. Acts 13:22, The Message.
11. Attributed widely to Lucille Ball (1911–89), American comedienne. http://www.famousquotes.com/show.php?_id=1013131. Accessed December 6, 2007.
12. Psalm 25:7, The Message.
13. "Butchers and Shepherds," www.clarion-call.org/yeshua/sheep/butchers.htm. Accessed July 6, 2007.
14. Eldridge, John & Stasi, *Captivating: Unveiling the Mystery of a Woman's Soul*, Nashville, TN: Thomas Nelson, 2005, p. 7.
15. Young, William P., *The Shack*, Calle Norte, CA: Windblown Media, 2007, p. 132.
16. Keller, Phillip, *A Shepherd Looks at the 23rd Psalm*, Grand Rapids, MI: Zondervan, 1970.
17. Jenkins, S., & Hodges, B. A., "Ram Kills Elderly Couple," *Salisbury Post Online*, November 6, 2000. www.salisburypost.com/2000nov/110600a.htm. Accessed January 13, 2006.
18. Joni Earickson Tada, talk at "Writing for the Soul" Conference, Colorado Springs, CO, 2004.
19. Psalm 140:7.
20. Griffiths, B. & Griffiths, C., *The Road to Forgiveness*, Nashville, TN: Thomas Nelson, 2001, pp. 169–75.
21. Chambers, Oswald, *My Utmost for His Highest*, New York: Dodd, Mead, & Co., 1935, devotion for August 4 entry.
22. Psalm 31:5, The Message.